Anonymous

Minutes of the Eighth Annual Meeting

of the General Executive Committee of the Woman's Foreign Missionary

Society of the Methodist Episcopal Church, held in the Centenary M.E.

Church, Minneapolis, May, 1877 - Vol. 1

Anonymous

Minutes of the Eighth Annual Meeting
*of the General Executive Committee of the Woman's Foreign Missionary Society of
the Methodist Episcopal Church, held in the Centenary M.E. Church, Minneapolis,
May, 1877 - Vol. 1*

ISBN/EAN: 9783337291198

Printed in Europe, USA, Canada, Australia, Japan

Cover: Foto ©Lupo / pixelio.de

More available books at **www.hansebooks.com**

MINUTES

OF THE

EIGHTH ANNUAL MEETING

OF THE

GENERAL EXECUTIVE COMMITTEE

OF THE

Woman's Foreign Missionary Society

OF THE

METHODIST EPISCOPAL CHURCH.

HELD IN THE

CENTENARY M. E. CHURCH, MINNEAPOLIS,

MAY, 1877.

DELAWARE, O.:
G. H. THOMSON, PRINTER, LAME'S BLOCK.
1877.

MINUTES

OF THE

EIGHTH ANNUAL MEETING

OF THE

GENERAL EXECUTIVE COMMITTEE

OF THE

Woman's Foreign Missionary Society

OF THE

METHODIST EPISCOPAL CHURCH.

HELD IN THE

CENTENARY M. E. CHURCH, MINNEAPOLIS,

MAY, 1877.

DELAWARE, O.:
G. H. THOMSON, PRINTER, LAMB'S BLOCK.
1877.

Printed by order of the General Executive Committee

MRS. W. G. WILLIAMS, Delaware, Ohio.
MRS. W. A. INGHAM, Cleveland, Ohio.

Publishing Committee.

———•—

The General Executive Committee is indebted to Mrs. Dr. William B. Davis, of Cincinnati, for the maps accompanying this Report. These maps were prepared and executed under the direction of Mrs. Davis, by the appointment of the Cincinnati Branch, for the last Annual Report of that Branch.

TABLE OF CONTENTS.

——o——

MINUTES.

---o---

The General Executive Committee of the Woman's Foreign Missionary Society of the Methodist Episcopal Church, commenced its eighth annual session in the Centenary Church, Minneapolis, Minnesota, on Thursday morning, May 10, 1877; Mrs. Prescott, of the Western Branch, presiding.

The session was opened with devotional exercises, and Mrs. Dr. Savage, of the Cincinnati Branch, led the Committee in prayer.

Mrs. Dr. Goodrich, of Minneapolis, made a most cordial address of greeting to the delegation; and Mrs. Taplin, of the New England Branch, made an appropriate response.

The roll of the Committee was called, and the following delegates answered to their names:

NEW ENGLAND BRANCH.—Mrs. C. P. Taplin, Mrs. D. Richards, Mrs. A. C. Trafton.

NEW YORK BRANCH.—Mrs. William B. Skidmore, Mrs. D. D. Lore.

PHILADELPHIA BRANCH.—Mrs. John F. Keen, Miss Matilda A. Spencer.

NORTHWESTERN BRANCH.—Mrs. J. F. Willing, Mrs. E. A. Hoag, Mrs. J. H. Bayliss.

WESTERN BRANCH.—Mrs. L. E. Prescott, Mrs. Angie F. Newman, Mrs. Mary C. Nind.

CINCINNATI BRANCH. — Mrs. W. A. Ingham, Mrs. W. G. Williams, Mrs. G. S. Savage.

BALTIMORE BRANCH.—Miss Isabel Hart, Mrs. J. P. Newman, Mrs. W. B. Leitch.

The following officers were elected: President, Mrs. Dr. C. G. Goodrich, of Minneapolis; Recording Secretary, Mrs. W. G. Williams, Cincinnati Branch; Assistants, Mrs. L. R. Hoskins, Budaon Mission, India, and Miss Alice M. Guernsey, of St. Cloud, Minnesota.

The Standing Committees were then appointed as follows:

On Publication.—Mrs. Williams, Mrs. Trafton, Mrs. Lore, Miss Spencer, Mrs. Nind, Mrs. Leitch, Mrs. Hoag.

On Finance.—Mrs. Skidmore, Mrs. Taplin, Mrs. Keen, Miss Hart. Mrs. Willing, Mrs. Ingham, Mrs. Prescott.

On Extension of Work.—Same as Committee on Finance.

On Missionary Candidates.—Mrs. Richards, Mrs. Savage, Mrs. Bayliss, Mrs. Angie F. Newman, Mrs. J. P. Newman.

The following was presented and adopted as the standing order of the day, viz.:

9 A. M. Devotional Exercises; 9:30 to 12:30, Business; 2 to 3 P. M., Devotional Meeting; 3 to 5, Committee Meetings; Wednesday evening, May 6, Anniversary; Monday morning, May 14, Discussion of Home Work.

The following ladies were appointed to lead the devotional meetings:

For Thursday afternoon—Mrs. Keen, Philadelphia Branch.
For Friday afternoon—Mrs. Savage, Cincinnati Branch.
For Saturday afternoon—Mrs Richards. New England Branch.
For Monday afternoon—Miss Hart, Baltimore Branch.
For Tuesday afternoon—Mrs. Lore, New York Branch.
For Wednesday afternoon—Mrs. Willing, Northwestern Branch.
For Thursday afternoon—Mrs. Skidmore, New York Branch.

The following resolutions were adopted:

Resolved, That the Standing Committees on Publication and on Missionary Candidates be invited to meet the Committee on Finance whenever their own work will allow; and that the Finance Committee have like invitation to the meetings of the Committees on Publication and on Missionary Candidates.

Resolved, That we provide for the reporting of the proceedings of this meeting in all our church papers.

Requests were made by the New York and the New England delegations, respectively, that Miss Sparkes be permitted a seat with the former, and Mrs. Daggett with the latter, which were granted.

The annual reports of the Corresponding Secretaries were presented, showing the receipts for the year as follows:

New England Branch.	$13.337 62
New York.	13.176 63
Philadelphia.	6.232 11
Northwestern.	14.770 43
Western.	8.139 40
Cincinnati.	12.282 47
Baltimore.	4.526 24
Total.	$72.464 30

Mrs. Taplin inquired, what should constitute a complete report of a Corresponding Secretary; and on motion, the Committee on Finance was instructed to consider and report on the subject.

Announcements were made, and the Committee adjourned until Friday, 9 A. M., with the benediction by Rev. Daniel Cobb, of Minneapolis.

SECOND DAY, FRIDAY, MAY 11.

The session opened at 9 A. M. The devotional exercises were conducted by Mrs. Nind, of the Western Branch.

By resolution, the introduction of the missionaries present was made the first order; and Rev. Mr. and Mrs. Hoskins and Miss Sparkes, of India, and Miss Porter, of China, were introduced, and spoke feelingly of their work, and of the good providence of God in raising up so efficient an instrumentality as the Woman's Foreign Missionary Society for carrying forward our Missionary enterprises; which was followed with prayer by Rev. Mr. Martin. of Minneapolis, for the special blessing of God upon his servants. and upon their labors, on their return to their respective fields.

Miss Porter was assigned a seat with the Western Branch delegation.

Letters were read extending invitations to the delegates to stop at Milwaukee and Evanston, on their return from Minneapolis, and assist in Missionary meetings; and they were referred to a special committee, consisting of Mrs. Taplin and Mrs. Bayliss.

A resolution prevailed that the Branches be arranged and called in the order of priority of organization, as follows: New England, New York, Philadelphia, North Western, Western, Cincinnati, Baltimore.

8

The Secretary of the Committee on Finance made a partial report, which was adopted.

[See Report of Committee on Finance.]

Mrs. Keen, on behalf of the Committee of Reference, a committee to which business is referred in the interval between the meetings of the General Executive Committee, presented a report of the items referred to it during the year, and the disposition made of them, as follows :

1. Miss Hart, Corresponding Secretary of the Baltimore Branch, wished to know whether her Branch should send Miss Swaney to Pachuca, Mexico, to which she had been assigned, after statements from Dr. Butler representing the superior claims of Guanajuato as a new field of labor for her services. The Committee reported adversely to taking the new work.

2. Mrs. Ingham, Corresponding Secretary of the Cincinnati Branch, asked that her Branch be allowed to recall Miss Mason on account of failing health. The Committee reported favorably, and Miss Mason was recalled.

3. Mrs. Keen, Corresponding Secretary of the Philadelphia Branch, forwarded the testimonials of Miss Mary F. Cary, recommending her as a missionary teacher to Bareilly, India. The Committee passed favorably upon these testimonials, and she was accepted.

4. Mrs. Taplin, Corresponding Secretary of the New England Branch, asked for the appointment of a treasurer for Peking, China, to act in the absence of Miss Porter, in America. The Committee made a temporary appointment.

The action of the Committee in each case was approved.

On the motion of Mrs. Willing, a committee of three was ordered to consider By-Law 6, and to propose such amendments as shall authorize final action by the Committee of Reference. Mrs. Willing, Mrs. Lore and Mrs. Nind were appointed such committee.

Mrs. Lore presented the following, which was referred to the special committee on revision of By-Law 6 :

Resolved, That hereafter notice of all business transacted by the Committee of Reference, that is of interest to the Society in general, be promptly forwarded for publication to the editor of the "Heathen Woman's Friend."

The committee to which was referred the letters of invitation from Milwaukee and Evanston, reported, through Mrs. Taplin, grateful acknowledgments for the cordial invitations, and regrets that the entire committee could not accept them. The Corresponding Secretary of the Northwestern Branch was, however, instructed to say that a delegation of ladies would try to make it convenient to visit Evanston upon adjournment.

Mrs. L. H. Daggett, the agent of the "Heathen Woman's Friend," made her annual financial statement, which was accepted and referred to the Committee on Publication.

[See Report of Committee on Publication.]

A communication from Mrs. Warren, editor of the "Heathen Woman's Friend," was read, accepted, and referred to the Committee on Publication.

The following was passed by a rising vote :

Resolved, That the General Executive Committee has listened with great pleasure to the communication of the editor of the "Heathen Woman's Friend," and that we hereby express our appreciation of the very efficient services rendered by Mrs. Warren, and deeply regret her absence from the Executive session, as we deem her presence essential to our interests.

The minutes of yesterday were read and approved.

Announcements for the afternoon and evening were made, and the Committee adjourned to Saturday, at 9 A. M., with prayer and benediction.

THIRD DAY, SATURDAY, MAY 12.

The Committee assembled at 9 A. M., and the devotional exercises were conducted by Mrs. Trafton, of the New England Branch.

The roll of the delegates was called, and the minutes of yesterday were read and approved.

Mrs. J. B. Hanson and Mrs. E. M. Williams, of Minneapolis, ladies representing the Congregational Board of Foreign Missions of the Interior, were introduced. Mrs. Hanson presented the greetings of her organization, and made a statement of facts in regard to the extent and character of its work, to which Mrs. Ingham, of the Cincinnati Branch, responded; after which all joined in singing,

"Blest be the tie that binds
Our hearts in Christian love;
The fellowship of kindred minds
Is like to that above."

Visiting ladies from Winona and Muscatine were introduced.

The Committee on Missionary Candidates, through its Secretary, Mrs. J. P. Newman, made a partial report, which was discussed and recommitted.

Reports from the foreign fields being the special order for the day, were next taken up, and in accordance with resolution 9 of the Report of the Committee on Finance for 1876, the ladies designated reported for the several fields.

1. INDIA.—Mrs. Skidmore reported for Rohilcund District, as follows :

The Bareilly Orphanage, originally supported by the parent Society, was given into our care in 1871, since which time Miss Sparkes has had charge until the present year, when Miss Cary succeeds her during her visit home. In 1876 the property was purchased by the Woman's Foreign Missionary Society for the sum of $6,500. Miss Sparkes' report gives the following interesting statistics: "We close the year 1876 with 154 girls in the Orphanage; 18 new ones have been received during the year, 19 have married and left us, and 3 have died; 22 have been received into full membership in the church, and 36 on probation. All received during the last year are young—none over 8 years. Of the three that died, two, Eva Miller and Naomi de Newark, left behind a good testimony of faith in Jesus, which leaves no doubt on our minds in regard to their future; the third was an infant of only a few days. During the year many of the older girls have been led to make a fuller consecration of themselves to God than ever before. Others have received new light and quickening, and still others have newly found the Savior."

The medical work in Bareilly has been in charge of Miss Green for the past year, and has been very successful. She reports the number of patients in Dispensary, 2,322; patients in Hospital, 26; visits to zenanas, 44; visits to native Christians, 26. Miss Green succeeds Miss Swain, whose labors for six years are well known, and who was the first medical lady missionary ever sent to Asia.

The Home occupied by the ladies is the residence presented by the Nawab of Rampore in 1872, to which has been added a complete Hospital building, which has proved an efficient aid to mission work.

The Zenana work in Bareilly is under the care of Mrs. Thomas, and the schools and native Christian women are in charge of Mrs. Waugh.

MORADABAD.

As a Society we are under great obligation to Mrs. Parker for her untiring zeal and direction of the work, particularly in the city of Moradabad. Here we have 12 schools, and 4 Bible women, 2 medical helpers and 1 medical student. The medical work is still under the care of Miss Lore, now Mrs. McGrew, who has visited over one hundred patients in their homes in the city, and prescribed for 1,174 patients in the dispensary, and in the mission compound an average of five patients daily has been attended to. The dispensary has been greatly benefitted by a grant-in-aid from the Government, and a new dispensary has been opened at Chandausi, thirty miles from Moradabad.

The Zenana work in Moradabad has been efficiently carried on by Miss Pultz during the past year, but failing health has made her return home necessary.

The new Home belonging to our Society is a pleasant residence, erected at a cost of $3,500. We also own the school building, valued at $2,000.

FROM BUDAON

We miss the excellent reports of Mrs. Hoskins, at present in this country; but the work has been carried on by the Bible women, under the direction of Brother Wheeler.

Mrs. Knowles superintends the schools, and reports that prejudice against the education of girls is being slowly removed. Mrs. McHenry has charge of the work in East Shahjehanpore and Panahpore. It is mainly among the children of native Christians, a most important work. She also superintends the Zenana and school work in Bijnour, where she resides. She says the most hopeful prospect of immediate success is in two villages near Bijnour, the result of earnest work on the part of a woman who was educated and converted in the Bareilly Orphanage.

Mrs. Prescott reported for Kumaon District:

At Nynee Tal the work has been nearly the same as last year, and the school has numbered about the same as for several years past, but an unusual interest has been manifested. At Pitorahgarh the girls' school has been kept up steadily. One of our Orphanages, located in Paori, in this district, was in charge of Miss Blackmar until January, 1877, when she was transferred to Lucknow.

Dr. Johnson, formerly Medical missionary at Nynee Tal, writes: "As to the importance of Paori as a Mission field, I think we have no place in India more promising. It is the head of the Province of Gurhwal, with a population of 318,000 souls. Paori is on the hill, in a good climate, and thickly settled neighborhood. You could count twenty villages from one standpoint. The people in the Province are less prejudiced and bigoted, and more ready to receive the message of salvation, than in the large cities. Missionaries in the Hills are deprived of many social privileges enjoyed in some of the large stations in the Plains; but the most successful missions in India have been, and are, in such localities. If we can find faithful laborers willing to settle among the Hill people, the converts will be ten in the Hills to one in the Plains."

At the beginning of the year there were five schools in Gurhwal. One has since been closed. The school in Srinugger is doing tolerably well, with an average attendance of twenty girls of good class, who are much attached to their teacher. Srinugger is six miles from Paori, down the river. There is a good road between them.

Some of the money sent for the medical work at Paori was spent in procuring medicine, which was used by Miss Blackmar for the treatment of ordinary ailments. The medicines were received in June, and before October forty cases were successfully treated.

Mrs. Ingham reported for Oudh District:

LUCKNOW.

This great and wicked city yields very slowly to the power of the Gospel. Two Zenana teachers, one city school visitor and six Bible-women are employed by the Woman's Foreign Missionary Society. Parents are indifferent to the education of girls, hence attendance upon the day schools is irregular. Early marriages interfere seriously with classes, and prevent securing permanent faithful teachers. The Sunday Schools are better attended; in some of these the Lesson Leaves have been used. Golden Texts and subjects committed to memory. The Hindustan Missionary Society meets regularly every month, and has contributed in mites the sum of Rs. 21 4-9 (sicca*). This has been set apart to buy books and tracts

* The gold rupee of Bombay and Madras is worth about $7. The silver rupee (sicca rupee), coined by the East India company at Calcutta, is worth a little more than 2s. sterling, or nearly $0.50.

for the zenanas. Among the attendants at the weekly prayer meetings are women strong in faith that their prayers will be answered, that they may yet see in Lucknow a vigorous and holy native church.

THE CHRISTIAN GIRLS' BOARDING SCHOOL.

Is becoming known throughout the Empire. Miss Isabella Thoburn, Superintendent, with six assistants, enrolled during the last year 137 pupils, of whom 65 board. One-third of the entire number are East-Indians. The school is quite free from caste-feeling. An appeal has been issued to the residents for funds wherewith to build cottages for self-boarders of high caste. So far but Rs. 545 have been received.

CAWNPORE.

A great work might be opened at this point were there any one to carry on the enterprise. Mrs. Mansell's death gave a temporary blow to usefulness here. The Cawnpore memorial school has been divided, and Miss Thoburn supervises the girls' department. It is a severe tax upon this eminent and devoted woman, and it is to be hoped that laborers for this part of the vineyard may ere long be sent forth.

At GONDAH, one or two girls' schools have been organized by the Government. Several little ones are learning to read, write and knit in their own homes.

At ROY BAREILLY are two schools, doing fairly. Angelina Barnabas and Salome Isa Dar are efficient Bible women, and report much good done in visitation among all classes.

At SEETAPORE is a girls' school and two Bible women.

An interesting Zenana school, for women whose husbands occupy positions in Government employ, has been opened at HURDUI.

Two schools have been kept up at BARABANKI. Mrs. Janvier, the naitve pastor's wife, has been teaching in several Baboos' families.

2. CHINA.—Mrs. Keen reported the Kiukiang work :

The work of the Woman's Foreign Missionary Society was commenced in Kiukiang in 1872 by the sending out of two missionaries, Miss Hoag and Miss Howe. During the last year the new building for school and home has been completed, at a marvelously small expenditure. This is, doubtless, owing to the young ladies' knowledge of native character, and their personal supervision of the work. The school numbers 21 scholars, of whom seven have been with our young ladies since the beginning. The assistant teacher is Mrs. Shoa, a native Chinese convert.

In this District it has rained most of the time for eight months; the Yang-tse overflowed it banks to a very unusual extent, and the lower floor of the old building, where Miss Hoag and Miss Howe resided, was under water for several months. This caused not only much additional labor in removing furniture and living entirely in the upper stories, but also much sickness. Several of the children, all the servants, and Miss Howe herself were ill. Finally it became necessary to leave the house, and accept the invitation of Mr. Cook to occupy his residence on the hill, which he vacated expressly to accommodate the sick family of our mission.

The Kung Lung school has prospered during the last year, has had twelve scholars, and is taught by Mrs. She. The money appropriated for a new building for this school has not been used, as the Parent Board concluded not to occupy Kung Lung as a new mission station at present. Mrs. She, who was converted through the labors of our young ladies, is the wife of a native helper, and has been employed as Bible-woman for the last four years. Our missionaries say she is one of the native Chinese who can be trusted, and is conscientious in the discharge of her duties.

Our faithful Bible-woman. Mrs. Tong, has been ill for several months, but is now again going from house to house "teaching the doctrines," as she calls her work, seeking to overcome prejudices, and persuading attendance at the school and chapel. There is a weekly prayer meeting among the girls at the school, which they very much enjoy, and anticipate with interest.

The time for adjournment having arrived, a motion prevailed to set aside the regular order for Monday until the completion of the reports from foreign fields.

Adjourned to 9 A. M. Monday. Dismissed with prayer by Miss Hart, and singing the doxology.

FOURTH DAY, MONDAY, MAY 14.

The devotional exercises were conducted by Mrs. Hoag, of the Northwestern Branch.

Notwithstanding the arduous duties in which most of the delegates were engaged on the Sabbath, on roll call no member was found absent. The minutes of Saturday were read and approved.

The special order, reports from foreign fields, was then taken up. China was continued, Miss Hart reporting for Foochow :

Our Mission work in Foochow consists of a Girls' Boarding School, Medical work, the support of 21 day schools, and 11 Deaconesses or Bible-women. Meetings for women are held weekly at each of the three Methodist churches, and a monthly meeting alternately at each.

The Boarding School, commenced in 1859, is under the care of the Misses Woolston, assisted by a native teacher. The present number of pupils is 31, of whom three also act as teachers. Fourteen are members of the church, of whom eleven were received on Christmas day, 1876. Thirty-three girls have graduated from the school, of whom six are now engaged in teaching day schools, and one is studying medicine.

The medical work is under the charge of Miss Sigourney Trask, M. D. During the year dispensary work has been carried on in a small building within the Mission Compound. The new Hospital is nearly completed. It is a commodious structure, 96 feet by 58, with two stories, combining residence for the Physicians with ample ward rooms for 40 in-patients, drug room, surgery, reception room, and rooms for native nurses and medical students. It will probably be formally opened about the 1st of March. The appropriation for purchasing a site and building the Hospital is $5,000. A few statistics of the medical work for 1876 are appended: No. of patients, 681; surgical operations, 58; visits to native houses, 273; prescriptions given, 1,243. Mrs. Baldwin writes that the Hospital building is well arranged and admirably adapted to its purpose, and will be of great service in our Mission work, as the medical work, and especially the dispensary practice, overcomes prejudice and opens the way to the hearts and the homes of the people. Dr. Trask is reported as efficient and popular, and is regarded by some of the natives as something more than human.

The twenty-one day schools, taught by native teachers, are under the supervision of the missionaries, as is also the work of the Deaconesses. We are under obligation to Mrs. Baldwin, Mrs. Sites, Mrs. Plumb and Mrs. Chandler, the wives of missionaries of the Parent Board, for efficient supervision of our native helpers, and co-operation in our work.

The Child's Paper is an important auxiliary in our work. It is attractively illustrated, and has a large circulation.

Mrs Taplin presented the report for Peking :

The work of the Woman's Foreign Missionary Society in this Mission commenced in the early part of 1872. Miss Maria Brown and Miss Mary Q. Porter were its first representatives. The growth of the work has not been rapid, but exceedingly encouraging. The school, which was opened soon after the arrival of the missionaries, has been continued with varying numbers and success, and not a little good seed has been scattered by this instrumentality. Seventeen girls are now enjoying the advantages of the school, and the instruction which by the blessing of God will, no doubt, result in their eternal salvation. Three of the school girls have become members of the church, and several others are earnestly seeking to do the will of the Master. Even those who stay but a short time, and go away apparently unchanged, carry with them seeds of truth which may yet spring up and bear much fruit. Meetings for women are held weekly, and into these come many who have never before heard of Christ. Several have given good evidence of conversion. One woman, now under the instruction of Mrs. Davis, comes several hundred miles that she may "learn of the doctrines," and be prepared to tell the wonderful story of the cross to her idolatrous neighbors.

An auxiliary to the Woman's Foreign Missionary Society has been formed, and the mites of missionaries and their wives, of converted Chinese women, and of the little school girls are given to send the Gospel to those who have not yet received it.

The medical work in Peking is one of the most efficient agencies in reaching the native women. Miss L. L. Coombs, M. D., went out in May, 1873, to open this branch of the work. She has been eminently successful in professional labors, and never fails to point her patients to the Great Physician.

Our present force in Peking is Miss L. A. Campbell, Miss Coombs, M. D., and Miss Leonora Howard, M. D., recently sent to join Miss Coombs in her medical work. Miss Porter, now at home for treatment of the eyes, expects to return the coming autumn.

The Woman's Foreign Missionary Society has in Peking real estate as follows:

Home and School, . .	$4.487 17
Hospital and Dispensary, .	5,621 82
Total,	. $10,108 99

This was supplemented with an interesting verbal report by Miss Porter, missionary at Peking. Letters were also read from Christian helpers. From one of the most striking, a letter from the Ku Cheng deaconess, Ting Chin Si, the following extract was ordered to be published. It was written to our missionary, and by her translated, preserving as far as possible the idioms of the Chinese :

This Quarter I have gone to my relatives' and friends' houses to sell books and to teach. I find that the people know to distinguish between good and evil. One day I was passing in front of a *greatly-believing-idols* man's house. A woman inside called me in and said, "Give you to see. Can the idols hear and answer?" I replied, "Have you not heard persons rebuking the lazy use the words, 'You are made of mud and wood?' If people who are *like* mud and wood are exceedingly useless and stupid, how much more the *real* mud and wood useless! Can that hear and answer?" The woman was immediately very angry and said, "Do you immediately go out of my house, and from this time let not your feet touch my door, and do not say those words again." This woman afterwards had a son, whom she consecrated or offered to an idol to secure its protection. The child sickened and died, and the woman's husband, being angry, took an axe and cut the idol in pieces; then the woman herself knew that the idols can neither hear nor answer. Unfortunately several other families had a share in this idol, and when they knew what the man had done they compelled him to have another idol made. Now this man and his wife hear me teach the doctrines, and desire to put away all bad customs. Another day I met a woman with several little children. She tried to compel me to go with her to an idol temple. That temple-god's name is "Tai po 'kung" (great protecting grandfather). The woman said, "If you dare to go to the temple, and, before this god's face, say he cannot hear and anwer, and he does not immediately punish you, then truly he has no power." There was no help for it but for me to go, and in the temple, before the idol, I told her the idol was only mud and wood and truly could not hear or answer. The woman seemed ashamed. She struck the bell and drum (found in most temples), and in a loud voice called on the idol for a half hour, but she heard nothing or perceived no benefit. She then said to me, "The Jesus you worship truly is very great. I will receive your words, and you teach me how to worship God." Among the women in the temple, about one-half seemed convinced of the truth. My whole heart was full of joy, and I thanked God who had given me patience and such a good opportunity for teaching the doctrines.

In regard to this Quarter's opportunities, some have blasphemed, some have slandered, and others have treated me with respect. I have remembered that the Lord's desire is to save this world's sinful men. Following this meaning, I dare not talk of grief-or-trouble's-business, only can tell this to my Lord Christ, trusting that he will cause that which I do work, and that which I speak words to glorify his death. This Quarter. *Ku-Cheng* church mothers and sisters all have peace, also exert themselves in their duty toward God; but there is one household, *Tong King's*, that, having received the doctrines, still are very weak. I have exhorted them many times, and also have asked members of our class to see and pray with them. Now I desire God to give grace that Ku-Cheng's so many church members may be like the flourishing grape vine, and not have any withered branches, but may bring forth much fruit and so glorify God. This my heart truly desires.   TING CHIN SI,
                                    Presents respectful salutations.

This was followed with the singing by Miss Porter, in Chinese, of the familiar Sabbath School hymn,

"When he cometh, to make up his jewels."

Most touching allusion being made by Mrs. Angie F. Newman, to the great sacrifice and sorrow of a mother in giving a daughter to go to foreign lands, the audience sang, with overflowing eyes,

"Were the whole realm of nature mine,
    That were a present far too small;
Love so amazing, so divine,
    Demands my soul, my life, my all."

3. SOUTH AMERICA.—Mrs. Willing read a report of our work in South America :

The work of our Society in South America is confined to the city of Rosario. We have two ladies there, Misses L. B. Denning and J. M. Chapin. They report decided progress, their school having increased from twelve to thirty-one pupils, some of whom give good evidence of being taught by the Holy Spirit the principles of the better life.

The priests teach the mothers that it is a mortal sin to send their children to a Protestant school; yet the women ridicule the idea, and keep their children in the school. Liberal sentiment seems to prevail in Rosario. Rev. Thos. B. Wood has care of the public instruction of the city; which would not be allowed if the Jesuits had their way. One woman told Miss Denning that in some places in the Argentine Republic, to say one was a Protestant would be the same as saying he was a demon.

Like most papist lands, it is sunk in such gross ignorance, it hopes for little, and has nothing to lose. The people count it no sin to steal from those who have more than one has himself; and vices of all kinds are winked at in faithful Catholics.

Our school there promises great good. One of the scholars, seven years old, is too advanced for her grandmother's school, though that is an institution of some consequence, and numbers fifty scholars. This small specimen of a missionary, this little seven-year-old, goes home from the Sunday School taught by our ladies, and teaches the girls in her grandmother's school to sing, "Come to Jesus," and other Spanish Sunday School hymns, while her schoolmates teach the same to their playfellows and mothers at home; and so the seed is scattered.

Our ladies have access to great numbers of women in their homes, talking and singing to them, praying for them, and pointing them to Christ. The women sit on the ground, smoking their cigars, and drinking their mate; yet they listen gladly and thankfully. As one poor soul said, "Nobody before ever cared to teach me so much as to say the Lord's Prayer, or to wash a kettle." Mrs. Wood, of Rosario, says of Miss Denning that she has rare capabilities as a missionary. She has shown marked ability in mastering the language, and in translating; and is untiring in her zeal. Miss Denning writes of herself: "I rejoice daily in the blessed privilege of walking in the light of God's countenance. His Spirit is leading me to more perfect trust in him as my all in all. His blood cleanses and keeps me at rest."

Mrs. Dr. D. D. Lore, who, with her husband, was for several years a missionary in Buenos Ayres, followed this report with some remarks concerning the wonderful change in the freedom of expression of opinion and of action since her residence there. Mrs. Willing called special attention to the fact that although Rosario is a Catholic city, Rev. Thomas B. Wood, a Methodist minister, has charge of its public school interests.

4. BULGARIA.—Mrs. Willing reported the work in Bulgaria:

No work is more carefully reported, and none promises larger results for the outlay than that in Bulgaria. It is impossible to tell how it may be hindered by the present war, as our field is near the frontier. Rustchuk, the headquarters of the Methodist mission, is one of the points on the Danube that are threatened by the Russians. We have assumed here the support of four native Bible-women. They are reported by the superintendent of the mission as most faithful and efficient. Their names are Clara Proca, Varvara Ivanof, Magdalena Elief and Kristina Todorf.

Superintendent Flocken writes that the prospect of a war with Russia, and the atrocities of the Turks, have so taken up the mind of the people that they hardly talk of anything else. At Lone Paleanka, where Magdalena Elief is at work, the native preacher has been obliged to leave his charge to attend to the war sufferers, but Magdalena keeps bravely at her Bible work through heavy persecutions and difficulties. She finds the superstitions of the people sadly in her way,—they believe so fully in enchantment and soothsaying. She has had trouble to find a house to live in, because she would not consent to let the Priest come and sprinkle it with holy water to drive out the evil spirits, as their custom is, the first of each month.

The priests have threatened the people to leave them all to the power of the bad spirits, if they do not take their children away from the Protestant schools; but Mr. Flocken says that he is of the opinion, that, as the priests are paid for their purification performance, they will be glad to attend to it, school or no school, when they find so many *piastres* less in their pockets at the end of each month.

5. MEXICO.—Mrs. Skidmore reported the missions in Mexico:

The work in Mexico is carried on by three ladies, Miss Susan M. Warner, Miss Mary Hastings and Miss Nettie Ogden. The first named lady is in charge of the Orphanage in the city of Mexico, which at present contains between forty and fifty girls, of whom twenty-four attend class meeting regularly, two are in full membership, seven were to be received in two months, and the rest remain on probation. The Berean Lessons form part of the work of the week, as well as of the Sunday School, and the children are improving constantly in every respect. It is a most interesting and useful work. Miss Warner is assisted by Miss Ogden.

In Pachuca, the capital of the State of Hidalgo, Miss Hastings has charge of a school for girls numbering forty Spanish and thirteen English pupils. During the revolution last autumn the city was bombarded twice, and the mission premises, being in the line of fire, suffered considerably. Ugly holes in the walls, and bullets embedded in chairs, give evidence that the mission family passed through great danger; but God was their defence, and not one received personal injury. The school has already been a blessing to many homes, parents being attracted to the religious services by the interest shown by their children, and some have been converted. Several of the girls have given evidence of sound conversion, and many attend class meeting regularly. We also support a Bible reader in Pachuca, who has made 487 visits during the past year, and distributed Bibles, portions of Bibles, and tracts, to the number of 783. The demand for tracts is greater than the supply.

The Orphanage in Mexico is valued at $2,000, and the Home at Pachuca at $2,000.

6. AFRICA.—Miss Hart made the report for Africa:

In Africa we have simply continued the work of former years, the support of a day-school, at an expense of $240. Despite frequent failures and peculiar difficulties, our church seems to have the deepening conviction that it has not done its whole duty in this quarter, and that we are bound to make further inquiry, looking to more intelligent, earnest and successful work in the future. And so a representative from our Episcopacy and one from our ministry have been visiting and examining with a view to our department of labor—school work.

Dro. Deputie, of the Liberia Conference, writes: "The Parent Missionary Society made a failure, in the early days of missions, by not getting girls and training them, in a country like this, where polygamy is practiced to such a fearful extent. The boys we raise will go to their people and to their kin to take their wives; and this has been peculiar to the human race since the days of Abraham. To secure a piece of land and establish a Home for the education of females, is the thing we greatly need. Let them be placed under the care of a good governess with assistants; let the teachers take the entire control of the children and place them under strict discipline, and the future will tell wonders on the redemption of Africa. To build a house and send out teachers will cost your Society a considerable sum of money, more perhaps than you are able to spare at this time; and yet I am convinced this is the most efficient plan that can be adopted to bring out beneficial results. Your school at Bexley is doing a good work as far as it goes, and so with all others established on a similar basis; but the great demand just now is training institutions to qualify teachers for the native work."

The offering of three well-worn gold rings to the Missionary cause by a colored woman in Liberia, whose heart God had touched, shows how responsive are some hearts in that dark land to Gospel claims.

It was stated that two educated young colored women had indicated their desire to enter the African mission field under the auspices of the Woman's Foreign Missionary Society, as soon as the way should be opened for them ; also that prosperous Auxiliary Societies are being organized in colored Methodist Episcopal churches.

7. JAPAN.—Mrs. Willing read a report of the work in Japan :

Japan is one of our most promising fields. Miss Schoonmaker and Miss Whiting are at last settled in their new home. Miss Schoonmaker writes of the building: "It is within the limits of the Foreign Concession. The location is most beautiful and healthful, and affords a lovely view of one of the finest bays in the country. It is a trial to give up the hope of being located outside of the Concession, among the natives; but with the knowledge I now have of Japanese character, I should not dare to advise buying property outside of the Concession. This will be the third, perhaps the fourth, Boarding-school in the Concession; but after a little hard work, I hope to establish a flourishing school here, and with Japanese helpers hope to be able soon to begin day schools in different sections of the great city of Tokio." She has now a scheme by which she hopes to reach the poor. She says: "Aside from the girls' school recently opened in Tokio by the liberality of the Empress, there are here at least two, and there soon will be three, schools conducted upon the plan which we have hitherto followed, reaching only the higher classes. You know what an immense city Tokio is; but I question whether you can have any adequate idea of the amount of misery, vice, and degradation prevailing here. You know of the depths of sin and suffering in some of our large cities at home, but what must be the case here, where asylums and benevolent institutions for alleviating suffering are almost unknown."

Of herself she says: "I shall thank God through all eternity for what He has taught me by the hard experience of the last year. Perplexities harass me, but I look up and say, 'My Father, lead me,' and peace like a river flows into my soul."

We are thankful that God has thus cared for our missionaries and their work. If we remember them in daily prayer, we know that the coming year will be far more abundant in results.

8. ROME.—Mrs. Taplin reported that as yet we have undertaken no work in Rome. She has been in correspondence with Dr. Vernon with reference to the practicability of assuming work there, and its character, which correspondence she was ready to present if desired. On motion, it was referred to the Committee on Extension of Work.

Adjourned to 9 A. M. Tuesday. Dismissed with singing and prayer by Mrs. Bayliss.

FIFTH DAY, TUESDAY, MAY 15.

The devotional exercises were conducted by Mrs. Power, of Muscatine, Iowa.

The roll was called, and the minutes of yesterday were read and accepted.

A telegram from Dr. Butler, of Mexico, was read, asking that the Committee continue its session until the arrival of an important communication then on its way from Mexico. Referred to the Committee on Extension of Work.

Mrs. Skidmore presented a letter of greeting and a report from Mrs. Parker, Corresponding Secretary of the India work. The following is an extract from the report :

The work of the past year has been finished, and we have entered upon the duties of the present year with new hopes, new purposes and new consecration. God is with us as never before. The Spirit convicts many of sin, and we are watching and waiting to see souls brought to Christ. The work in its several departments was carried forward as usual during the year, and most of the laborers were able to remain at their posts of labor.

You will mourn with us in the loss of our dear sister Mansell, who was with us so short a time. She came with a heart full of love for the people of this land, and did what she could for them while strength was given. When God called her she went with joy and triumph to receive the plaudit. "Well done, good and faithful servant."

Three Bible-women, also, have entered into rest, leaving abundant testimony that there is power in the religion of Jesus to give victory in the hour of death. Two of our sisters have gone to America, and may, perhaps, with others of our missionaries who are at home, be present with you at your meeting. Miss Sparkes was appointed our delegate, and, with the others who may be able to be with you, will give you much information concerning our work.

As the printed report of our work for the past year will be in your hands, I do not need to repeat what is written there, but will give you a brief summary of the work which you are supporting here. There are four ladies here, and three at home, who have been sent out and supported by the funds of the Society. Miss Thoburn has commenced her eighth year of labor in the country. She has charge of two important interests in our work,—the Lucknow Christian Girls' Boarding School, and the Cawnpore School for English-speaking girls. Miss Blackmar has charge of the Zenana work in Lucknow, and she is also devoting some time to the writing and translation of books specially adapted to the work in the girls' schools and zenanas. Miss Green is in charge of the medical work in Bareilly, which was so successfully inaugurated by Miss Swain. Miss Cary has charge of the Girls' Orphanage in Bareilly. Miss Swain, Miss Sparkes and Miss Pultz are in America, and we hope they may do much there to aid you in your work.

There are seven East-Indian ladies employed by the Society,—four in Lucknow and three in Bareilly. These are very efficient helpers in our work, and we look to the new school in Cawnpore to furnish us with more of this class of helpers. There are three medical Bible-women and two medical students in connection with the work in Bareilly and Moradabad, who are doing efficient work both as doctors and Zenana teachers. There are in all our mission more than seventy Bible-women teaching in many houses and exerting an influence over many minds. Ten Christian women are employed specially as teachers in schools. You have, therefore, more than one hundred Christian agents here, besides a large number of married women, American and native, who are in charge of work which you are supporting. There are two girls' Orphanages, where about one hundred and seventy girls have a Christian home and the advantages of a Christian education. There are three Christian girls' boarding schools, besides the one just opened in Cawnpore, in which there are one hundred and sixty girls. There are seventy-eight schools for Hindoo and Mohammedan girls, in which there are one thousand four hundred and fifty-six girls. These are all taught the principles of Christianity, and there are many Sunday Schools in connection with these schools.

From this brief summary, which I have made out as carefully as I could, you will see that the work which you have in hand is one of such magnitude that you can hardly have a true conception of its importance. So many agencies at work among the millions of Oudh and Rohilcund must result in great good. The labors of so many going forth daily "bearing precious seed," and "sowing beside all waters," attended by the spirit of all truth, must in time bring forth fruit to God's glory.

At the close of the report Miss Hart offered the following, which was passed:

Resolved. That we have heard the communication from Mrs. Parker with great pleasure, and return to her and her fellow-workers our most cordial greetings.

That part of Mrs. Parker's report which related to taking up new work was referred to the Committee on Extension of Work.

The President called on Miss Sparkes, missionary from Bareilly, India, to make some statements concerning the character and work of the East-Indian women employed by our Society. Miss Sparkes responded quite at length, and in doing so spoke very highly of the Christian character, faithfulness and ability of these valuable helpers in our mission work, and of their superior intelligence which everywhere commands the respect of the heathen natives.

The report of the Committee on Finance was called. A partial report, referring especially to the duties of Corresponding Secretaries, was presented, which, after discussion and amendment, was adopted, as found in the report of the Committee on Finance.

[See Report of the Committee on Finance.]

At 12 o'clock a motion to adjourn prevailed, the members going into committee work till 12:30, when lunch was announced.

SIXTH DAY, WEDNESDAY, MAY 16.

The devotional exercises were conducted by Mrs. Prescott, of the Western Branch.

After roll call, the minutes of yesterday were read and approved.

Mrs. Bayliss, of the Northwestern Branch, stated that tidings from home made it necessary for her to ask to be excused, at the close of the morning session, from further duty as delegate. She was so excused.

In view of the necessity for her absence, Mrs. Bayliss further requested that the report of her committee (Committee on Missionary Candidates) be made the first order of business, which was granted. Mrs. J. P. Newman presented the report, which was accepted, discussed, amended and passed.

[See Report of the Committee on Missionary Candidates.]

Mrs. Angie F. Newman stated that she had memorials referring to extension of work, which she would like to present at the proper time; and they were referred without reading to the Committee on Extension of Work.

Mrs. Prescott presented the following, which was adopted:

WHEREAS, The Western Branch of the Woman's Foreign Missionary Society has Auxiliary Societies of strength in Wyoming Territory; and, WHEREAS, the Western Branch, through its Corresponding Secretary, hereby requests the General Executive Committee to extend the geographical boundaries of our work so as to embrace this territory; therefore,

Resolved, That Wyoming Territory be included within the bounds of the Western Branch.

A partial report of the Committee on Publication, referring especially to the "Heathen Woman's Friend," was presented by Mrs. Williams, discussed, amended and passed.

[See Report of the Committee on Publication.]

Adjourned to meet at 9 A. M. Thursday. Dismissed with singing and benediction.

Anniversary Meeting, Wednesday Evening, May 16.

The Eighth Anniversary of the Woman's Foreign Missionary Society was held in Centenary church ; Rev. Daniel Cobb, pastor of the church, presiding. The devotional exercises were conducted by Rev. Mr. Hoskins, missionary in India.

The following statistical information was submitted by Mrs. Williams, Secretary of the General Executive Committee :

There are now in the whole organization 2,196 auxiliaries; annual memberships, 53,438; honorary patrons, managers and life members, 1,443. Amount of money raised during the past year, from February 10, 1876, to February 10, 1877, $72,464.30. Since the beginning of the Society in 1869 the total receipts have reached $379,800. Our results in foreign fields are thus estimated: "During this time we have sent missionaries to all the countries occupied by the parent Board, except Europe and Africa; and at one station in each of these, Bulgaria and Bassa, we are employing native Bible women. There have been sent to foreign fields thirty young ladies as missionaries. Five of these have left our work; four to remain in the same calling as wives of missionaries, and one to take professional employment under the government in India, we trust still to be a teacher of the Gospel. Five ladies have returned on furlough. Those remaining in the field are working with rare efficiency and success. We have introduced medical work into Asia through five of our ladies. Under their direction one dispensary and three hospitals have been built. Besides the Orphanage in Bareilly, India, and the Girls' Boarding School in Foochow, China, which we received from the parent Board, two Orphanages, one in Paori, one in the city of Mexico, and six buildings for homes and boarding schools have been erected in the different stations occupied. We have supported the work carried on by the wives of missionaries, besides employing 140 Bible women, native teachers and other helpers, and are sustaining at least 130 day schools."

Three young ladies have been sent out during the year: Miss Mary F. Cary, of Fishkill, N. Y., educated at Lima, sailed for Bareilly, India, in September, 1876; Miss Olivia Whiting, of Jasper, N. Y., educated also at Lima, sailed August 15, 1876, for Tokio, Japan; Leonora Howard, M. D., from Grand Rapids, Mich., educated at Michigan University at Ann Arbor, sailed April 15, 1877, for Peking, China.

This report was followed with remarks from the returned missionaries present, Misses Sparkes and Porter, and Mr. Hoskins. Stirring missionary speeches were made by Rev. Mr. Cobb and Mrs. Nind.

Miss Hart displayed to the audience three well worn rings, and told the following incident in regard to them : They had been the property of a native African woman in Liberia. Under the preaching of the Gospel she had become so filled with zeal to do good that when Bishop Haven was in Liberia, she gave these rings to him, saying that they were precious mementoes which she could not see worn upon a strange hand in her own country; but she would be glad to have him bring them to his country, and dispose of them as he thought best for missionary purposes.

At the close of Miss Hart's remarks, $110 were contributed to make this far-off woman, "whose heart God had touched," an Honorary Life Manager of the Woman's Foreign Missionary Society of the Methodist Episcopal Church.

All the exercises were interspersed with excellent singing of appropriate hymns by the choir of the church, and native hymns by the missionaries present. The church was filled to its utmost capacity, and much interest was developed. The "Heathen Woman's Friend" was not forgotten; a statement being made of its condition, value, and prospects, and an appeal to all present to become subscribers, and to prevail upon others to subscribe for it.

SEVENTH DAY, THURSDAY, MAY 17, 1877.

The devotional exercises were led by Rev. Mr. Hoskins.

The roll was called, and the minutes of yesterday were read and accepted.

The Committee on Publication presented a partial report, which was accepted, discussed, amended and adopted.

[See Report of the Committee on Publication.]

A partial report of the Committee on Finance was presented, discussed and adopted.

[See Report of the Committee on Finance.]

Mrs. Nind made some announcements concerning boat arrangements for return; when a motion prevailed to adjourn. The doxology was sung, and the benediction pronounced by Rev. Mr. Hurd, of Minneapolis.

EIGHTH DAY, FRIDAY, MAY 18.

The devotional exercises were conducted by Mrs. Richards, of the New England Branch.

The Committee on Publication presented a partial report, part of which was referred to the Committee on Finance, and a part recommitted.

On the motion of Mrs. Willing, the following was adopted:

Resolved, That the Committee on Publication be requested to consider the desirability of publishing, in the volume of Proceedings of this meeting, a short historical sketch of the Society, covering the points that are most frequently subjects of inquiry among our workers.

On motion, adjourned for committee work.

Ninth Day, Saturday, May 19.

The devotional exercises were conducted by Mrs. J. P. Newman.

After the half hour assigned to devotional exercises, the Finance Committee was excused from the session, in view of the pressure of work upon the committee.

The morning was devoted to the consideration of the home-work of the Society. Plans for conducting meetings, organizing auxiliaries, and raising funds were discussed; difficulties were stated, and methods of obviating them presented; many touching incidents of personal experience were related; and all felt encouraged and strengthened for another year of labor and sacrifice.

Adjourned to 2 p. m.

Afternoon Session.

Opened with singing, and prayer by Mrs. Daggett..

The final partial report of the Committee on Publication was presented, discussed, amended, and passed; and the report was adopted as a whole, and the committee discharged.

[See Report of the Committee on Publication.]

The amendments to the Constitution, proposed last year, were considered and adopted item by item.

[See Minutes of General Executive Committee for 1876, pp. 12 and 13.]

Mrs. Skidmore was asked to state what action had been taken by the committee appointed to confer with Doctors Dashiell and Reid, the Secretaries of the Parent Board, with reference to a joint report of our work with that of the General Missionary Society. She replied that the committee presented the report of the Woman's Foreign Missionary Society for joint publication, to the Secretaries in New York; but that no resolution instructing them to publish it was found upon the Journal of Proceedings of the General Conference, consequently they did not feel themselves authorized to assume the responsibility of a joint publication.

A committee, consisting of Mrs. W. B. Skidmore, Mrs. W. F. Warren and Mrs. W. G. Williams, was appointed to confer with the Missionary Secretaries, in regard to the publication of the statistical report of the Woman's Foreign Missionary Society in connection with the report of the General Missionary Society.

Mrs. Willing offered the following, which was adopted:

Resolved, That we commend the pleasant and sprightly manner in which Mrs. M. B. Willard has conducted the Children's Corner of the "Friend," and we would respectfully recommend the continuance of that department under her care.

The following was adopted :

Resolved, That we appreciate the presence of the returned missionaries, Mr. and Mrs. Hoskins, and Misses Sparkes and Porter ; and most sincerely thank them for their timely and efficient service and hearty co-operation in our work, and assure them of our sympathies and prayers in all their future labors at home and abroad.

The following resolution, offered by Miss Hart, was passed, and ordered to be printed in the next issue of the "Heathen Woman's Friend" :

Resolved, That the Woman's Foreign Missionary Society of the Methodist Episcopal Church would hereby pay an affectionate and reverential tribute to the memory of Mrs. T. C. Doremus, known and honored not only as the originator of the Woman's Foreign Missionary Society in this country, but as one of the most beautiful specimens of Christian womanhood and intense devotion to Christian work that have adorned and blessed the century, her name being as sweet ointment poured forth, filling all churches and all lands with its perfume.

Mrs. Taplin presented an invitation from the Executive Committee of the New England Branch to the General Executive Committee to hold its next annual meeting in the city of Boston. The invitation was accepted.

On the motion of Mrs. Hoag, it was ordered that the Historical sketch of the Society, prepared for the minutes, be also published as a leaflet.

The following were appointed a Committee on Publication of Leaflets, Tracts, etc. :

New England Branch,		Mrs. L. H. Daggett.
New York "	}	Mrs. J. T. Gracey.
Philadelphia "	}	
Northwestern "		Prof. Sue M. D. Fry.
Western "		Mrs. Mary C. Nind.
Cincinnati "		Mrs. W. G. Williams.
Baltimore "	. .	Miss Ella Kelly.

Mrs. J. T. Gracey was made chairman of this committee, with power to choose her own secretary from members of the committee.

The following were elected as Editorial Contributors to the "Friend" :

New England Branch,		Mrs O. W. Scott.
New York	"	Mrs. Dr. Olin.
Philadelphia	" .	Mrs. Stephen P. Darlington.
Northwestern	"	Mrs. Jennie F. Willing.
Western	" .	Mrs. Angie F. Newman.
Cincinnati	"	Mrs. W. A. Ingham.
Baltimore	" . .	Miss Isabel Hart.

Mrs. Nind gave notice of the following proposed amendments of the Constitution :

Article V., Section 1, to strike out "two delegates" and insert "one delegate"; also, to strike out "which delegates together with two reserves," and insert "which delegate together with one reserve."
Article IX., to strike out "of each Branch delegation."

Mrs. Skidmore announced the receipt of a communication from Dr. Butler ; and it was referred, without reading, to the Committee on Finance.

The following resolutions were passed :

Resolved, That the thanks of this body are tendered to the Secretary of the Northwestern Branch, for her services in securing special railroad rates to delegates; and to the ladies of Chicago for the entertainment of delegates en route to Minneapolis.

Resolved, That the thanks of this body are tendered to the President of the Chicago, Milwaukee and St. Paul Railroad; and to Commodore Davidson, President of the Northern Packet Line, for special rates over their respective routes of travel.

Resolved, That our thanks are tendered the trustees and pastor of the Centenary Methodist Episcopal Church, for the use of the church and parsonage during the session; and to the citizens of Minneapolis, for the bountiful and graceful entertainment afforded us, in the noonday lunches; in the delightful excursions, and in the warm welcome to their hospitable homes.

Resolved, That the thanks of this body are tendered to Mrs. C. G. Goodrich, the president, for her courteous and impartial discharge of duty ; and to the secretaries for their faithful and efficient services.

Upon motion, adjourned to 8 P. M. Dismissed with singing, "Praise God from whom all blessings flow."

EVENING SESSION.

The meeting was called to order by Mrs. Willing. Mrs. Hoag was chosen president pro tem. Mrs. Richards led in prayer.

Mrs. Willing presented the final partial report of the Committee on Finance, which was discussed and passed ; and the report was adopted as a whole, and the committee discharged.

[See Report of the Committee on Finance.]

The estimates for the coming year were passed.

[See Appropriations for 1877-78.]

Mrs. Willing, chairman of the committee to which was referred the modification of By-Law 6, reported the following items to be added:

If it is deemed necessary to recall a missionary during the year, it shall have power to order her return.

If the office of treasurer in a foreign mission field becomes vacant during the year, it shall have power to fill the office.

The report was adopted.

Adjourned, to meet at 9 A. M. Monday.

TENTH DAY, MONDAY, MAY 21.

The session was opened with singing, and prayer by Mrs. W. G. Williams.

The minutes of the entire meeting of the General Executive Committee, together with the reports of the standing committees, were read and approved; and directions were given in regard to their publication.

Mrs. Daggett, agent of the "Heathen Woman's Friend," was instructed to contract for the publication of 16,000 copies.

The following resolutions were adopted:

Resolved, That the General Executive Committee of the Woman's Foreign Missionary Society of the Methodist Episcopal Church gratefully recognizes the magnanimous Christian action of the Maryland Annual Conference of the Methodist Protestant Church in its cordial reception of the representatives of our Society, and in its subsequent resolution ordering that during the coming year a collection be taken in every appointment of their Conference for the work of this Society.

Resolved, That the General Executive Committee hereby requests the Branches within whose bounds the annual meetings of the Woman's Board of Missions, and of similar organizations of other church, may be held, to appoint suitable delegations to bear to these co-workers in the Master's vineyard the cordial greetings of the Woman's Foreign Missionary Society of the Methodist Episcopal Church.

Resolved, That the abstracts of foreign reports, which appear in the minutes, be submitted to the Leaflet Committee for early publication as leaflets.

Some closing remarks were made by the President, Mrs. Dr. Goodrich, which were responded to by Mrs. Keen.

Prayer was offered by Mrs. Skidmore, after which all joined in singing,

"And if our fellowship below
In Jesus be so sweet;"

and the Committee adjourned *sine die*.

MRS. WILLIAM G. WILLIAMS,
Secretary.

REPORTS OF COMMITTEES.

———o———

No. 1.

REPORT OF THE COMMITTEE ON PUBLICATION.

1. *Resolved*, That we consider the HEATHEN WOMAN'S FRIEND an indispensable auxiliary to our work; that we most earnestly commend its interests to the care and the prayers of all our women; and that we respectfully suggest that our official ladies regard it their duty to present its claims whenever our cause is represented.

2. *Resolved*, That each Branch delegation nominate one editorial contributor for the coming year.

3. *Resolved*, That we recommend that the Corresponding Secretaries be responsible for all contributions to the Home Department of the FRIEND.

4. *Resolved*, That the fiscal year of the FRIEND correspond with that of the other financial interests of our Society.

5. *Resolved*, That the Agent of the FRIEND be requested to make to each Branch Corresponding Secretary a Quarterly Report of the number of subscribers in each Branch, together with a list of expired subscriptions, arranged by Conferences, on the tenth of May, August, and November, and an annual itemized report on the tenth of February to the standing Committee on Publication.

6. WHEREAS, The following causes are assigned for the great decrease in our number of subscribers to the FRIEND, viz.: 1st. Financial depression, which has led our workers, unconsciously to themselves, to press the claims of membership to the neglect of subscriptions to the paper; 2nd. The peculiar circumstances of the past year, owing to Centennial and political interests, which have absorbed the attention of our ladies; 3rd. Cutting off subscribers immediately upon the expiration of the time of subscription; 4th. The delay in the receipt of the paper; therefore

Resolved 1. That we urge our women to seek to secure subscribers to the FRIEND in every Methodist family.

Resolved, 2. That papers be sent to subscribers two months after the expiration of subscriptions.

Resolved, 3. That the Branch Corresponding Secretaries call the attention of the Corresponding Secretaries of Auxiliaries to their duties in this direction as defined in By-Laws for Auxiliaries No. 4.

Resolved, 4. That we pledge ourselves, as delegates; to secure, if possible, our proportion of twenty thousand subscribers, from July 1st, 1877, according to the ratio of our membership.

Resolved, 5. That we have carefully examined the itemized report of the Agent of the FRIEND, and are satisfied that the paper has been managed with economy and untiring devotion to its interests.

7. *Resolved,* That the thanks of the Society are due Mr. J. P. Magee, for his kindness in auditing the accounts of the FRIEND for the past year, and that we shall gratefully accept the same service for the coming year.

8. *Resolved,* 1. That Mrs. W. F. Warren, Editor of the FRIEND, has given entire satisfaction, and we recommend her employment as Editor for the ensuing year at a salary of five hundred dollars, with stationery and postage from the proceeds of the paper.

2. That we further recommend the employment of Mrs. L. H. Daggett as Agent and Publisher of the FRIEND, at a salary of six hundred dollars, with stationery and postage from the proceeds of the paper.

3. That if, in the judgment of the Committee on Publication, the financial condition of the FRIEND warrant it, the traveling expenses of the Editor and Agent, to the General Executive Committee meeting, be paid from the proceeds of the paper.

9. *Resolved,* That the Editor of the FRIEND be instructed not to hold the manuscript for the paper later than the 15th of each month.

10. *Resolved,* That we recommend that the Committee on Publication consider the propriety of publishing a full and accurate history of the Woman's Foreign Missionary Society, for the first ten years of its existence, and, if found practicable, that the volume be completed and on sale at our Decennial Meeting, 1879.

11. *Resolved,* That we recommend the publication of 700 copies of the Minutes of the Eighth Annual Meeting of the General Executive Committee, including the Constitution and By-Laws, Record of Missionaries, and a short Historical Sketch of the Society, covering the points which are most frequently subjects of inquiry with new workers; each Branch pledging itself to take its proportionate share of copies so printed.

12. *Resolved,* That the Committee on Publication of Minutes be instructed to secure the most favorable terms of publication possible.

MRS. W. G. WILLIAMS,
Miss MATILDA A. SPENCER,   CHAIRMAN.
Secretary.

————O————

No. 2.

REPORT OF THE COMMITTEE ON MISSIONARY CANDIDATES.

1. *Resolved,* That the testimonials of Miss Laura F. Ray, Lafayette, Indiana, are perfectly satisfactory, and we hereby recommend her as entirely competent to the Foreign Missionary work in any field that may be assigned her.

2. *Resolved,* That the testimonials of Miss Mary Clayland, Bridgeport, Ohio, are entirely satisfactory, and that we recommend her as fully qualified for usefulness in any field in our Foreign Missionary work.

3. WHEREAS, The compounding of medicines makes the work of a medical missionary very laborious, and requires much time ; and, WHEREAS, we learn from reports received through letters and returned missionaries that assistants are desired, and in cases of surgical operations are sometimes absolutely necessary, therefore.

Resolved, That your Committee recommend that assistants be furnished wherever practicable.

4. WHEREAS, Much of the special preparatory work of our missionaries must be done at present in foreign countries, and under the depressing influences of a debilitating climate, thereby injuring their future usefulness; and, WHEREAS, our returned missionaries are amply qualified to instruct

candidates in all the requirements for foreign service; therefore,

Resolved, That we will provide at home, as soon as is practicable, and as far as is practicable, such training as will fit them for their duties in the foreign field.

5. *Resolved*, That some experienced medical practitioner be selected in each Branch, who shall be shown the health certificate of each candidate after it has been filled out by a physician, and who shall give an opinion as to her physical capabilities, and to what climate her constitution is best adapted.

6. *Resolved*, That a copy of the following requirements of the Woman's Foreign Missionary Society be furnished each missionary candidate by the Secretary of the Branch to whom application is made, upon the presentation of such application:

a. A missionary candidate must believe herself divinely called to the work of a foreign missionary.

b. She must present a certificate of health from a competent physician, and give satisfactory answers to the medical questions authorized by the General Executive Committee of the Woman's Foreign Missionary Society.

c. She must furnish satisfactory testimonials of thorough scholarship.

d. We regard financial and executive ability, and power of adaptation to circumstances, as *essential* qualifications; and some experience in teaching, and knowledge of medicine and nursing, as *desirable* qualifications for all ladies in our employ as missionaries.

e. The age of a missionary candidate must not be less than twenty-two nor more than thirty. A thorough intellectual training, with a facility for the acquisition of languages and a remarkable ability for Christian work, may be considered a sufficient reason for some deviation from strict adherence to this rule.

f. Though her preference will be considered, she must cheerfully accept any field of labor to which she may be assigned.

7. *Resolved*, That the following be adopted, to-wit:

SPECIAL CONDITIONS UNDER WHICH MISSIONARIES ARE EMPLOYED BY THE WOMAN'S FOREIGN MISSIONARY SOCIETY OF THE METHODIST EPISCOPAL CHURCH.

1. All missionaries in the employ of the Woman's Foreign Missionary Society will labor under the direction of the authorities of the Missionary Society of the Methodist Episcopal Church, and be subject to the rules and regulations which govern the other missionaries of the Methodist Church where they may be stationed in their legitimate work.

2. They will be expected to devote their entire time and attention to their legitimate work, as all their temporal necessities will be provided for by the Society.

3. They are required to send annual and quarterly reports to the Corresponding Secretary having charge of their work; and the action of the General Executive Committee will be communicated to them through that Secretary or the correspondent appointed for their field by said committee, and no other instructions are to be considered as official.

4. They are especially requested to include in their reports all items, anecdotes, and incidents that are suitable for publication in the "Heathen Woman's Friend."

5. They, with the wives of missionaries who labor in the interest of this Society, shall constitute a committee to prepare at each session of the Conference or annual meeting of the missionaries, the estimates for the ensuing year, which estimates shall have the sanction of said Conference or annual meeting before being forwarded to the General Executive Committee.

6. They shall incur no expense during the year to be met by this Society, for which the estimate has not previously been submitted to and approved by the General Executive Committee at its annual meeting.

7. They shall credit to the Society all donations received for the support of their work, and annually report the same with their financial statement.

8. A medical missionary shall be accountable to the Branch from which she is sent. She shall keep an itemized account of all receipts and disbursements; such receipts may be used for necessary expenses in her medical work, any surplus being credited to her Branch.

9. Every missionary employed by this Society is required to give at least five years' continuous service as a single woman to the mission work assigned her; and should she, for any reason (sickness excepted), withdraw from the work of the Society before the expiration of that term, she will be required to refund the amount expended for her outfit and passage.

10 The Society agrees to pay the expenses of its missionaries from their homes to their places of destination, their salaries to date from the time of their arrival in the mission field; if a missionary be obliged to relinquish her work temporarily on account of ill health, the Society agrees to meet the expense of her return, and pay her a salary of $500 for the first year thereafter; if she continue in the work of the Society in America, her traveling expenses will be paid by the Branch that employs her.

11. Every lady employed by this Society is required to signify her willingness to accept the above conditions by signing her name thereto.

MRS. E. S. RICHARDS,
CHAIRMAN.

MRS. J. P. NEWMAN,
Secretary.

———o———

No. 3.

REPORT OF THE FINANCE COMMITTEE.

1. *Resolved*, That "By-Law 4" be amended by inserting as item 6 in the order of business "Report of the Committee of Reference."

2. *Resolved*, That we add to the order of business the following item: "Reports of Standing Committees, daily, immediately after the Reading of the Minutes."

3. *Resolved*, That all Branch Treasurers be required to publish each month, in the "Heathen Woman's Friend," their report of money received.

4. *Resolved*, That each Corresponding Secretary be required to comprehend, in her report to the General Executive Committee, the following items: No. of Auxiliary Societies; No. of members; No. of life members; No. of honorary managers; No. of patrons; No. of subscribers to the "Heathen Woman's Friend."

5. *Resolved*, That in her report of foreign work she include the No. of missionaries; No. of assistant missionaries; No. of Bible-readers; No. of day schools; No. of boarding schools; No. of orphans supported by her Branch, with any personal notes that she may see fit to present in regard to them.

6. *Resolved*, That other information in regard to our Mission fields be presented in the reports of official correspondents.

7. *Resolved*, That, with a view to the organization of the Atlanta Branch, we appoint Mrs. G. S. Savage, of Kentucky, to the work of organizing Auxiliaries in Tennessee, North Carolina, South Carolina, Alabama, Georgia and Florida.

8. *Resolved*, That, with a view to the organization of the New Orleans

Branch, we appoint Mrs. J. P. Newman to a similar work in Arkansas, Mississippi, Louisiana and Texas.

9. *Resolved,* That a blank be prepared for our missionaries in the field, specifying the items required for our Annual Reports, and any other statistical information necessary; the blanks to be filled out and returned to the Corresponding Secretaries sending them, by March 1st of each year.

10. *Resolved,* That each Branch bear its part of the expense of this printing, *pro rata.*

11. *Resolved,* That Mrs. Taplin, of Vermont, be a Committee to prepare and publish said blank.

12. *Resolved,* That it be the duty of the Recording Secretary of the General Executive Committee to forward to the Treasurers in the foreign fields, as soon as practicable after adjournment, a copy of the appropriations for each Mission station.

13. WHEREAS, The Corresponding Secretaries are permanent members of the General Executive Committee; therefore,

Resolved, That we amend the By-Laws by inserting, as By-Law 9, the following, defining duties of Corresponding Secretaries:

The Branch Corresponding Secretaries shall superintend all the interests of their respective Branches; shall conduct the correspondence of the Society with foreign missionaries; shall be present at all Branch quarterly meetings and present a quarterly report of the work of the Branch, and shall give to the public, or direct to be given, all communications and plans of the business of their respective Branches.

14. *Resolved,* That all Conference Secretaries report quarterly to the Branch Executive Committee through their respective Corresponding Secretaries.

15. *Resolved,* That all correspondence of importance or special interest received from foreign fields be forwarded to the official correspondent before the time of the annual meeting of the General Executive Committee; and that from it she make such a digest as shall enable her to give a comprehensive view of the work under her charge, with any additional fact or feature of special interest.

16. *Resolved,* That the medical work in Kiukiang be left unprovided for for the coming year. Also that the medical outfit of Dr. Mason be left in care of Miss Hoag, with permission to dispose of the medicines if practicable.

17. *Resolved,* That since Miss Swain continues in too poor health to return to India, and is still receiving medical aid with a view to doing so, the New England Branch be allowed to pay her a salary of $500 for the coming year.

18. *Resolved,* That the Society refund to Rev. T. B. Wood, of Rosario, South America, two hundred dollars house-rent paid by him for our ladies in 1874; the money to be taken from "Balance on hand."

19. *Resolved,* That five hundred dollars be appropriated to Africa; the official correspondent for Africa directing as to place and purpose in and for which the money shall be expended.

20. *Resolved,* That the ladies in Kiukiang be allowed to draw from the surplus now in their treasury, paid by the Philadelphia and New York Branches, for the erection of a small building for sanitary purposes.

21. WHEREAS, Miss Mary Q. Porter has given five years of very satisfactory service in Peking, China, and after a year of rest finds her health sufficiently restored to return to her work; therefore,

Resolved, That we recommend her reappointment to the same field of labor.

22. *Resolved,* That the Treasurer be instructed to forward the May remittances upon the basis of the preceding year.

23. *Resolved,* That the following persons act as Treasurers for this

Society in the foreign fields: India, Mrs. Parker; Peking, Miss Campbell;
Kiukiang, Miss Hoag; Foochow, Mrs. Baldwin; Bulgaria, Rev. F. W.
Flocken; Africa, Rev. J. Deputie; South America, Rev. T. B. Wood;
Mexico, Mrs. Dr. Butler; Italy, Mrs. Dr. L. M. Vernon; Japan, Miss
Schoonmaker.

24. *Resolved*, That the Funds of the Woman's Foreign Missionary Society be entirely under the control of the General Executive Committee,
to be used only for the purposes designated at the General Executive Committee Meeting; any surplus funds in the hands of Treasurers in foreign
fields to be used for work already provided for by the General Executive
Committee.

25. *Resolved*, That assistant teachers in schools under the supervision
of the missionaries of the Woman's Foreign Missionary Society be under the
direction and employment of said missionaries, who shall be responsible
to their Society for the work and expenditures of such assistants.

26. *Resolved*, That each Corresponding Secretary be expected to report to the General Executive Committee the amount of provisional fund
expended by her Branch during the year, and the object for which it was
used.

27. *Resolved*, That in case any Branch is unable to meet the obliga-
tions it has assumed, any other Branch may, by the action of its Executive Board, be permitted to use its surplus funds in aid of the Branch de-
ficient.

28. *Resolved*, That the Treasurers of the several Branches be instructed to send their appropriations directly to their Treasurers in the foreign
field.

29. *Resolved*, That this General Executive Committee do most posi-
tively discountenance the organization of juvenile missionary societies
auxiliary to the Woman's Foreign Missionary Society, or the raising of
money in any way which violates the eighth article of our Constitution.

30. *Resolved*, That the money arising from annual membership shall
not be used for making life members, such members to be made by the
payment of twenty dollars specifically for that purpose, and their membership to be acknowledged at the time of subscription, and the payment of
the first five dollars.

31. *Resolved*, That all money save that paid for annual membership may
be used to make life members, honorary managers, or honorary patrons.

32. *Resolved*, That we cannot consider the proposition to take up work
in Utah, as it is contrary to both the spirit and the letter of our Constitution.

33. *Resolved*, That the Corresponding Secretary of the New England
Branch be instructed to correspond with Montevideo and ascertain the
help desired in that mission, and report to the Committee of Reference the
result of the correspondence.

34. *Resolved*, That if the Committee of Reference approve, the New
England Branch be permitted to appropriate thereto six hundred dollars
of its provisional fund.

MRS. WM. B. SKIDMORE,
CHAIRMAN.

MRS. JENNIE F. WILLING,
Secretary.

APPROPRIATIONS FOR THE YEAR
1877-'78.

———o———

INDIA.

ROHILCUND DISTRICT.

Bareilly.—

Orphanage,	$2,750
City Girls' School,	150
Christian Girls' School,	60
Bible-women,	360
Medical work,	384
Miss Swain's salary,	500
" Green's "	600
" " Incidentals,	150
" Bond's salary,	420
" Cary's "	600
" " Incidentals,	150
Miss Pultz's salary,	500
Miss Sparkes' return to India,	700
" " salary,	500
Khera Bajhera Girls' School and Bible-women,	150
Mrs. Piyari Banerjea,	180

Moradabad.—

Bible-women,	$400
Medical work,	300
Assistants,	150
Girls' School,	600
City Schools,	310
School Matron and Assistants,	240
Traveling Expenses,	50

Sumbhal.—

Girls' School and Bible-women,	$200

Bijnour.—

Schools and Bible-women,	$436
Two Scholarships,	36

Chandausi.—
    Bible-woman, $50
    Medical work,   50
Budaon,   650
Shahjehanpore,   280
Panahpere and *East Shahjehanpore,*   360
Amroha,   250
    Total,   ——$12,516

KUMAON DISTRICT.

Paori.—
    Orphanage, $384
    Boarding School,   45
    Srinugger Girls' School,   95
    District work   70
    Pithoragarh,   60
Nynee Tal.—
    Girls' School and Bible-woman, $200
    Total,   —— 854

OUDH DISTRICT.

Lucknow.—
    Miss Isabella Thoburn's Salary, $600
    " " " Incidentals   150
    " L. E. Blackmar's Salary,   600
    " " " Incidentals,   150
    " " " Traveling Expenses,   50
    " Duncan's Salary,   300
    " Mispelaar's "   300
    " Rowe's "   360
    Bible-women,   360
    Agnes Doherty,   60
    Miss Heming,   420
    Medical Lady to be sent,   1,500
    Lucknow School Buildings,   1,000
    Scholarships in Lucknow School,   270
    City Girl's School,   400
Cawnpore.—
    Purchase of Normal School property,   6,000
    Sending Lady to take charge of School,   1,500
    Girls' School and Bible-women,   200
Seetapore.—
    Girls' School and Bible-women,   150
Barabanki,   100
Gondah,   480
Hardui,   120
Roy Bareilly,   300
    Total,   —— 15,370

CALCUTTA.

Two Teachers to be sent, $1,600
    Total,   —— 1,600

    Total for India,   . $30,340

CHINA.

Foochow.—

Miss S. H. Woolston's Salary, . .			$600
" " " Incidentals, .			150
" " " Personal Teacher, .			72
" " " Traveling Expenses,			40
Miss E. Woolston's Salary, . . .			600
" " " Incidentals, .			150
" " " Personal Teacher,			36
" " " Traveling Expenses,			40
Boarding School, ...			800
" " Repairs, . . .			45
Eleven Day Schools, (Misses Woolston,)			880
Two Deaconesses, . . .			48
Miss S. Trask, M. D.—Salary, . .			600
" " " Incidentals, . .			150
" " " Personal Teacher, . .			72
" " " Traveling Expenses,			15
Hospital Expenses, . . .			725
" " Medical Students, .			48
Seven Deaconesses, . .			168
Three Day Schools, . .			240
Two to be opened, .			160
Postage, Stationery, etc., (Mrs. Baldwin,) .			8
Five Day Schools, . . .			400
Two to be opened, .			160
Three Deaconesses, . . .			72
Traveling Expenses, (Mrs. Sites,)			20
Two Day Schools, . . .			160
Two to be opened, .			160
Three Deaconesses, . . .			72
Traveling Expenses, (Mrs. Plumb,)			15
Two Day Schools, (Mrs. Ohlinger,) .			160
One Day School, (Mrs. Chandler.) .			80
Insurance, $39; Watchman, $42, .			81
Total, ...			—— $7,927

Peking.—

Miss L. Howard, M. D.—Salary, .			$600
" " " Incidentals, .			150
" " " Personal Teacher,			120
Hospital Expenses, ...			600
Miss Mary Q. Porter,—Salary, .			600
" " " Incidentals, .			150
" " " Personal Teacher, . .			60
" " " School Expenses, . .			300
" " " Traveling Expenses, return to China, . . .			700
" Letitia A. Campbell,—Salary, . .			600
" " " Incidentals, . .			150
" " " Personal Teacher, . .			120
" " " School Expenses, .			300
" " " Cart Hire, .			50
" " " Watchman, . .			54
" " " Repairs, . .			100
" L. L. Coombs, M. D.—Salary, .			600
" " " " Incidentals, . .			150
" " " " Personal Teacher,			120
Total, ...			—— 5,524

Kiukiang.—
Miss Gertrude Howe.—Salary,	$600
" " " Incidentals,	150
" Lucy H. Hoag.—Salary, .	600
" " " Incidentals;	150
Personal Teachers for both, .	110
Boarding School, .	650
Matron,	50
Gateman,	48
Orphans, .	150
Kung Lang School,	120
Bible-women, (Mrs. Tong and Mrs. She,)	100
Total, .	2,728

Total for China, $15,279

JAPAN.

Tokio.—
Miss Schoonmaker's Salary,	$600
" " Incidentals,	150
" Whiting's Salary, .	600
" " Incidentals,	150
Personal Teachers for both, .	240
Two Teachers, .	180
Twenty Scholarships, .	800
Bible-woman,—Salary, .	15
" Traveling Expenses,	15
Rent, Repairs, etc., .	250
Matron, .	60
Cook, .	48
Watchman, .	72
Total,	$3,276

Yokohama.—
Teacher, .	$72
Bible-woman,	60
Rent, .	60
Incidentals, .	10
Traveling Expenses,	25
Total, .	227

Hakodati.—
Bible-woman,	36

Total for Japan, $3,539

AFRICA.

Bexley, Bassa Co.—
School Work, .	$500
Total for Africa, .	$500

BULGARIA.

Mrs. Clara Proca's Salary and School Expenses,	$200
Bible-woman & Student in School, . . .	200
Total for Bulgaria, . .	$400

ITALY.

Rome.—

Three Bible-women, . .	$900
One " " provisional,	300
Total, . . .	$1,200

Venice.—

One Bible-woman,	300
Total for Italy,	$1,500

SOUTH AMERICA.

Rosario.—

Miss Chapin's Salary, .	$600
" " Incidentals,	150
" " Rent, .	450
" Denning's Salary, .	600
" " Incidentals,	150
" " Rent, . .	450
Total for South America,	$2,400

MEXICO.

Mexico City.—

Miss Warner's Salary, .	$600
" " Incidentals,	150
" Ogden's Salary, .	500
Personal Teacher, . .	120
Orphans and Orphanage,	3,100
School Requisites,	60
Bible-woman, (Ameca Mecca,)	180
Total, . .	$4,710

Pachuca.—

Miss Hastings' Salary,	$600
" " Incidentals,	150
Mexican Assistants, .	192
Rent, . . .	140
School Requisites,	180
Porter, . . .	90
Bible-woman,	60
Requisites, ...	70
Miss Swaney's Outfit, Passage and Salary,	1,150
Total, ...	2,632
Total for Mexico, .	$7,342

APPROPRIATIONS BY BRANCHES.

——o——

New England Branch.

India.

Moradabad. Christian Girls' School,	$600	
" City Girls' School,	310	
" Bible-women,	340	
" School Matron and Assistant,	240	
" Traveling Expenses,	50	
Bareilly, Miss Green's Salary,	600	
" " Incidentals,	150	
" Medical Work,	300	
" Orphanage,	300	
Bijnour, Schools and Bible-woman,	436	
Budaon,	650	
Amroha,	250	
Roy Bareilly,	300	
Mrs. Banerjea's Salary,	180	
Miss Swain's Salary,	500	
Cawnpore, School Building,	3,000	
Total,		$8,206

China.

Peking. Miss Campbell's Salary,	$600	
" " " Incidentals,	150	
" " " Personal Teacher,	120	
" School,	300	
" Cart-hire and Watchman,	104	
" Repairs,	100	
" Hospital Expenses,	300	
Total,		1,674

Japan.

Tokio, Support of Four Girls,	$160	
Yokohama, Teacher,	72	
" Bible-woman,	60	
" Incidentals and Traveling Expenses,	35	
" Rent,	60	
Total,		387

South America.

Rosario, Miss Chapin's Salary,	$600	
" " " Incidentals,	150	
" Rent,	450	
Total,		1,200

Mexico.

Mexico City, Orphanage,	$400	
" " Bible Woman, (Ameca Mecca,)	60	
" " School Requisites,	60	
Total,		520
Provisional Fund,		1,000

Total for New England Branch, $12,987

NEW YORK BRANCH.

India.

Bareilly, Girls' Orphanage,	$800	
" Miss Sparkes' Salary,	500	
" " Pultz' "	500	
" City Girls' School,	150	
" Christian Girls' School,	60	
" Bible-women,	360	
" Miss Sparkes' Return to India,	700	
Lucknow, Scholarships in Boarding School,	60	
" Bible-women,	180	
" Agnes Doherty,	60	
Moradabad, Bible-women,	60	
" Medical Work,	300	
" Assistants in Medical Work,	150	
Hurdui,	120	
Calcutta, Teacher to be sent,	800	
Total,		$4,800

China.

Foochow, Miss Trask's Salary,	$600	
" " " Incidentals,	150	
" " " Personal Teacher,	72	
" " " Traveling Expenses,	15	
" Hospital Expenses,	725	
" Four Deaconesses, (Mrs. Baldwin)	96	
" Incidentals, (Mrs. Baldwin,)	8	
Total,		1,666

Mexico.

Pachuca, Miss Hastings' Salary,	$600	
" " " Incidentals,	150	
" Four Months' Rent,	140	
" Requisites for New School,	180	
" Bible-woman,	60	
" Books, Tracts, etc.,	70	
" Porter,	90	
Mexico City, Orphanage,	800	
Total,		2,090

Japan.

Tokio, Miss Whiting's Salary,	$600	
" " " Incidentals,	150	
" " " Personal Teacher,	120	
Total,		870

Bulgaria.

Clara Preca and School,	$200	
Total,		200

Italy.

Rome, Bible-woman, (Mrs. Gay,)	$300	
Total,		300
Provisional Fund,		500
Total for New York Branch,		**$10,426**

PHILADELPHIA BRANCH.
India.

Paori, Orphanage,	$100	
Bareilly, Orphanage,	300	
" Miss Cary's Salary,	600	
" " Incidentals,	150	
Lucknow, City Girls' School,	400	
" Miss Heming's Salary,	420	
" Medical Lady to be sent,	1,500	
Cawnpore, Girls' School and Bible-woman,	200	
Total,		$3,670

China.

Peking, Miss Coombs' Salary,	$600	
" " " Incidentals,	150	
" " " Personal Teacher,	120	
Kiukiang, Boarding School,	600	
" Bible-women, (Mrs. Tong and Mrs. She,)	100	
Kung Lung School,	120	
Orphan,	50	
Foochow, Three Day Schools, (Misses Woolston,)	240	
" Two " " (Mrs. Ohlinger,)	160	
Total,		2,140

Japan.

Hakodati, Bible-woman, (Mrs. Harris,)	$36	
Total,		36

Mexico.

Mexico City, Girls' Orphanage,	$200	
Total,		200
Provisional Fund,		500
Total for Philadelphia Branch,		**$6,546**

42

NORTHWESTERN BRANCH.

India.

Paori, Orphans.	$180
Chandausi, Bible-women,	50
" Medical Work,	50
Bareilly, Orphans,	360
Lucknow, Miss Rowe's Salary.	360
" Scholarships,	90
Calcutta, Teacher to be sent,	800
Total.	—— $1,890

China.

Foochow, Miss S. H. Woolston's Salary.	$600
" " " " Incidentals,	150
" " " " Traveling Expenses.	40
" " " " Personal Teacher.	72
" Three Deaconesses. (Mrs. Baldwin.)	72
" Three Day Schools. "	240
" Two " " to be opened, (Mrs. Baldwin)	160
Peking, Miss Howard's Salary,	600
" " " Incidentals.	150
" " " Personal Teacher.	120
" Hospital Expenses.	300
Kiukiang, Miss Howe's Salary.	600
" " " Incidentals.	150
" Miss Hoag's Salary,	600
" " " Incidentals.	150
" Personal Teachers for both,	110
" Boarding School.	50
" Matron for Boarding School.	50
" Orphans.	100
" Gateman.	48
Total.	—— 4,362

South America.

Rosario, Miss Denning's Salary.	$600
" " " Incidentals.	150
Total,	—— 750

Bulgaria.

Bible-woman and Student in School.	$200
Total.	—— 200

Japan.

Tokio, Miss Schoonmaker's Salary.	$600
" " " Incidentals.	150
" " " Personal Teacher.	120
" Four Scholarships.	160
Total.	—— 1,030

Africa.

School Work.	$100
Total.	—— 100

Mexico.

Pachuca, Mexican Assistants.	$192	
Mexico City, Orphanage.	300	
" " Teacher, (Ameca Mecca,)	120	
Total,		612

Italy.

Rome, Bible-woman, (provisional,)	$300	
Total,		300
Provisional Fund.		500

Total for Northwestern Branch, $9,744

WESTERN BRANCH.

India.

Paori, Orphanage.	$104	
" Boarding School.	45	
Srinugger, Girls' School.	95	
Petorahgarh,	60	
District Work.	70	
Sumbhal, Girls' School and Bible-women.	200	
Khera Bajhera, Girls' School and Bible-women.	150	
Bareilly, Orphanage.	480	
Lucknow, Miss Blackmar's Salary.	600	
" " Incidentals.	150	
Seetapore, Girls' School and Bible-women.	150	
Gondah.	480	
Traveling Expenses.	50	
Cawnpore School Building.	1,000	
Total,		$3,634

China.

Foochow, Day School, (Misses Woolston.)	$80	
" Two Day Schools, (Mrs. Plumb,)	160	
" " " " to be opened.	160	
" " Deaconesses, (Mrs. Plumb.)	48	
" One " to be employed, (Mrs. Plumb.)	24	
" Traveling Expenses, (Mrs. Plumb,)	15	
" Watchman,	42	
Peking, Miss Porter's Salary.	600	
" " " Incidentals.	150	
" " " Travel'g Expenses, to return to China.	700	
" " " Personal Teacher.	60	
" School Expenses,	300	
Total.		2,339

Japan.

Tokio, Four Scholarships.	$160	
" Matron.	60	
" Cook.	48	
" Watchman.	72	
" Teacher for Native Schools.	100	

Tokio, Translation Teacher,		80
" Fuel and Lights for School,		96
" Rent of Mission Property,		200
" " " Chapel,		20
" House Repairs,		30
" Bible-woman,		15
" Traveling Expenses,		15
Total,	——	896

South America

Rosario, Rent,	$450	
Total,	——	450

Africa.

School Work,	$100	
Total,	——	100

Mexico.

Mexico City, Orphanage,	$200	
Total,	——	200

Italy.

Rome, Bible-woman,	$300	
Total,	——	300
Provisional Fund,		500

Total for Western Branch,		$8,419

———

CINCINNATI BRANCH.

India.

Lucknow, Miss Thoburn's Salary,	$600	
" " " Incidentals,	150	
" " Duncan's Salary,	300	
" " Mispelaar's Salary,	300	
" School Buildings,	1,000	
" Bible-women,	180	
" Five Scholarships,	120	
Bijnour, Two Scholarships,	36	
Cawnpore, Purchase of Normal School Property,	2,000	
" Sending Teacher,	1,500	
Bareilly, Orphanage,	360	
Shahjehanpore,	280	
Panahpore and East Shahjehanpore,	360	
Barabanki,	100	
Total,	——	7,286

China.

Foochow, Five Schools, (Mrs. Sites,)	$400	
" Two to be opened, (Mrs. Sites,)	160	
" Three Deaconesses, " "	72	
" Traveling Expenses, " "	20	
" Insurance,	39	
Total,	——	691

Japan.

Tokio, Four Scholarships.	$160	
Total.		160

Africa.

School Work.	$100	
Total.		100

Italy.

Venice, Bible-woman,	$300	
Total,		300

Mexico.

Mexico City, Miss Warner's Salary,	$600	
" " " Incidentals,	150	
" " " Ogden's Salary,	500	
" " " Personal Teacher,	120	
" " Orphans and Orphinage,	1,000	
Total,		2,370
Provisional Fund,		1,000
Total for Cincinnati Branch.		**$11,967**

BALTIMORE BRANCH.

India.

Nynee Tal. Girls' School and Bible-women,	$200	
Bareilly, Orphanage,	150	
" Mrs. Bond's Salary,	420	
" Medical Assistant,	84	
Total,		854

China.

Foochow, Miss B. Woolston's Salary,	$600	
" " " " Incidentals,	150	
" " " " Traveling Expenses,	40	
" " " " Personal Teacher,	36	
" Boarding School,	800	
" Repairs,	45	
" Medical Students,	48	
" Seven Day Schools, (Miss Woolston,)	560	
" One Day School, (Mrs. Chandler,)	80	
" Two Deaconesses, " "	48	
Total,		2,407

Japan.

Tokio, Four Scholarships.	$160	
Total.		160

Africa.

School Work.	$200	
Total.		200

Italy.

Rome, Bible-woman. $300
    Total.   .   .   ———— 300

Mexico.

Mexico City, Orphanage. $200
Pachuca, Miss Swaney's Passage and Salary,   1,150
    Total.   .   .   .   .   .   ———— 1,350
Provisional Fund.   200

        Total for Baltimore Branch. $5,471

SUMMARY.

	INDIA.	CHINA.	JAPAN.	AFRICA.	BULGARIA.	ITALY.	SO. AMERICA.	MEXICO.	PROVISIONAL.	TOTALS.
New England Branch,	$8,206	$1,674	$387				$1,200	$520	$1,000	$12,987
New York "	4,800	1,666	870	$200	$300			2,090	500	10,426
Philadelphia "	3,670	2,140	36					200	500	6,546
Northwestern "	1,890	4,362	1,030	$100	200	300	750	612	500	9,744
Western "	3,634	2,339	896	100		300	450	200	540	8,419
Cincinnati "	7,286	691	160	100		300		2,370	1,000	11,907
Baltimore "	854	2,407	160	100		300		1,350	200	5,471
Totals, ...	$30,340	$15,279	$3,559	$500	$400	$1,500	$2,400	$7,312	$4,200	$65,500

APPENDIX.

MISSIONARIES OF WOMAN'S FOREIGN MISSIONARY SOCIETY.

Date of Appt.	MISSIONARIES.	POST-OFFICE ADDRESS.	BRANCHES.	FORMER RESIDENCE.
1869	Miss Isabella Thoburn.	Lucknow, India.	Cincinnati.	St. Clairsville, O.
"	Clara A. Swain, M. D...	Home on leave.	New England.	Castile, N. Y.
1870	Fannie J. Sparkes.	Home on leave.	New York.	Binghamton, N. Y.
1871	Beulah Woolston.	Foochow, China.	Baltimore.	Trenton. N. J.
"	Sarah Woolston.	Foochow, China.	Northwestern.	Trenton. N. J.
"	Mary Q. Porter.	Home on leave.	Western.	Davenport, Iowa.
1872	Gertrude Howe.	Kiukiang, China.	Northwestern.	Lansing, Mich.
"	Lucy H. Hoag.	Kiukiang, China.	Northwestern.	Milan. Mich.
"	Lou E. Blackmar.	Lucknow, India. ..	Western.	West Springfield, Pa.
"	L. M. Pultz.	Home on leave.	New York.	Windsor, N. Y.
1873	Lucinda L. Coombs, M D.	Peking, China.	Philadelphia.	Cazenovia, N. Y.
1874	Susan M. Warner.	City of Mexico, Mexico, No. 5 Calle de Gante.	Cincinnati.	Groton, N. Y.
"	Mary Hastings.	Pachuca, Mexico.	New York.	Blanford, Mass.
"	Jennie M. Chapin.	Rosario, Argentine Republic. South America.	New England.	Chicopee, Mass.
"	Lou B. Denning.		Northwestern.	Normal, Ill.
"	Sigourney Trask, M. D..	Foochow, China.	New York.	Spring Creek, Pa
"	Dora Schoonmaker.	Tsukiji, Tokio, Japan. No. 10 Aktas-cho.	Northwestern.	Morris, P.
1875	Letitia A. Campbell.	Peking, China.	New England.	Cambridge, Mass.
1876	Lucilla H. Green, M. D..	Bareilly, India.	New England.	Lambertville. N. J.

Year	Name	Post-office Address		Supported by
1876	Miss Nettie C. Ogden.	City of Mexico, Mexico, No. 5 Calle de Gante.	Cincinnati.	Springfield, O
"	" Mary F. Cary.	Bareilly, India.	Philadelphia.	Fishkill, N. Y.
"	" Olive Whiting.	Tsukiji, Tokio, Japan, No. 10 Akasebo.	New York.	Jasper, N. Y
1877	" Leonora Howard, M. D.	Pekiva, China.	Northwestern.	Grand Rapids, Mich.
—	" Ellen Mispelaar.	Lucknow, India.	Cincinnati.	East Indian.
—	" Lydia Duncan.	Lucknow, India.	Cincinnati.	East Indian.
—	" Phebe Rowe.	Lucknow, India.	Northwestern.	East Indian.
—	" Caroline Fleming.	Lucknow, India.	Philadelphia.	East Indian.
—	" —— Bond.	Bareilly, India.	Baltimore.	East Indian.
—	Mrs. Piyari Banerjea.	Bareilly, India.	New England.	Hindoustanee

Missionaries Formerly Employed.

Year	Name	Post-office Address		Supported by
1871	Miss Carrie M'Millan.	Mrs. Rev. P. M. Buck, Gettysburgh, Pa.		Parent Society.
"	" Maria Browne.	Mrs. Rev. G. R. Davis, Peking, China.		Parent Society.
"	" Jennie Tinsley.	Mrs. Rev. J. W. Waugh, Bareilly, India.		Parent Society.
1873	" S. F. Leming.	Health failed. Returned May, 1871.		Sent by Cincinnati Branch
"	" Naomie Monelle.	Gone into Government service. Hyderabad, India.		Sent by New York Branch.
1874	" Lettitia Mason, M. D.	Health failed. Returned Aug., 1876.		Sent by Cincinnati Branch.
"	" Anna Julia Lore, M. D.	Mrs. Rev. P. H. M'Grew, Moradabad, India.		Parent Society.

TREASURERS IN THE FOREIGN FIELD.

———o———

INDIA.—Mrs. E. W. Parker, Moradabad, India. N. W. P., *via* Brindisi (Italian Mail).

PEKING —Miss L. A. Campbell, Peking, China, *via* San Francisco.

KIUKIANG.—Miss Lucy Hoag, Kiukiang, China, *via* San Francisco.

FOOCHOW.—Mrs. E. E. Baldwin, Foochow, China, *via* San Francisco.

BULGARIA.—Rev. F. W. Flocken, Rustchuk, Bulgaria.

AFRICA —Rev. J. Deputie, Liberia, Monrovia, Africa.

MEXICO.—Mrs. Dr. Butler, No. 5 Calle de Gante, City of Mexico, Mexico, per Steamer.

ITALY.—Mrs. Rev. L. M. Vernon, 126 Via Sistina, Rome, Italy.

JAPAN.—Miss Dora Schoonmaker, No. 10 Akas-cho, Tsukiji, Tokio, Japan.

SOUTH AMERICA.—Rev. T. B. Wood, Rosario, Argentine Republic, South America.

———

NOTE.—Letters sent to countries mentioned on the preceding pages, should be directed as follows :

To China and Japan, *via* San Francisco.
To India, *via* Brindisi (Italian Mail).
Mexico, per Steamer.

After June 1. 1877, all places of destination by routes above given become part of the General Postal Union, formed by the Treaty of Berne, and are subject to the following rates of Postage:

		ARGENTINE CONFEDERATION	
For Prepaid Letters, (½ oz.)	10 cts.		(British Mail).
For Postal Cards,	04 "	Letters (½ oz.),	27 cts.
For Newspapers (4 oz),	04 "	Newspapers, (2 oz.),	04 "
For Books, Patterns, Music, Photographs, Catalogues, etc., (2oz),	04 "	MEXICO, by land routes,	03 "

We are indebted to Mr. JOSEPH H. BLACKFAN, Superintendent of Foreign Mails, Washington, D. C., for the foregoing accurate postal rates.

CONSTITUTION.

——:o:——

Article I.—Name.

This Association shall be called "The Woman's Foreign Missionary Society of the Methodist Episcopal Church."

Article II.—Purpose.

The purpose of this Society is to engage and unite the efforts of Christian women in sending female missionaries to women in the foreign mission fields of the Methodist Episcopal Church, and in supporting them and native Christian teachers and Bible-readers in those fields.

Article III.—Membership.

The payment of one dollar annually shall constitute membership, and twenty dollars life membership. Any person paying one hundred dollars shall become an Honorary Manager for life, and the contribution of three hundred dollars shall constitute the donor an Honorary Patron for life.

Article IV.—Organization.

The organization of this Society shall consist of a General Executive Committee, Co-ordinate Branches and Auxiliary Societies, to be constituted and limited as laid down in subsequent articles.

Article V.—General Executive Committee.

Section 1. The management and general administration of the affairs of the Society shall be vested in a General Executive Committee, consisting of the Corresponding Secretary and two delegates from each Branch, which delegates, together with two reserves, shall be elected at the Branch annual meetings, said meetings to be held within two months before the meeting of the General Executive Committee. Said Committee shall meet at Boston the third Wednesday in April, 1870, and annually or oftener thereafter, at such time and place as the General Executive Committee shall annually determine.

Sec. 2. The duties of the General Executive Committee shall be : 1. To take into consideration the interests and demands of the entire work of the Society, as presented in the reports of Branch Corresponding Secretaries, and in the estimates of the needs of mission fields ; to ascertain the financial condition of the Society ; to appropriate its money in accordance with the purposes and method herein indicated ; to devise means for carrying forward the work of the Society ; fixing the amounts to be raised ; employing new missionaries, designating their fields of labor, examining the reports of those already employed ; and arranging with the several Branches the work to be undertaken by each. 2. To appoint a Committee, consisting of one from each Branch, to have charge of the missionary paper of the Society, and to arrange with the Corresponding Secretaries for the publication of an Annual Report of the work of the Society. 3. To transact any other business that the interests of the Society may demand, provided all the plans and directions of the Committee shall be in harmony with the provisions of the Constitution.

Article VI.—Branches.

Section 1. The organizations already formed at Boston, New York, Philadelphia, Chicago and Cincinnati, shall be regarded as co-ordinate Branches of this Society on their acceptance of this relationship under the provisions of the present Constitution.

Sec. 2. Other Branches may be organized in accordance with the following general plan for districting the territory of the Church :

Districts.	States.	Headquarters.
I.	New England States,	Boston.
II.	New York and New Jersey,	New York.
III.	Pennsylvania and Delaware,	Philadelphia.
IV.	Maryland, District of Columbia, and Virginia,	Baltimore.
V.	Ohio, West Virginia, and Kentucky,	Cincinnati.
VI.	Illinois, Indiana, Michigan, Wisconsin.	Chicago.
VII.	Iowa, Missouri, Kansas, Minnesota, Nebraska and Colorado,	Des Moines.
VIII.	Arkansas, Mississippi, Louisiana and Texas.	New Orleans.
IX.	Tennessee, North Carolina, South Carolina, Alabama, Georgia, Florida,	Atlanta.
X.	Pacific Coast.	San Francisco.

This plan, however, may be changed by an affirmative vote of three-fourths of the members of the General Executive Committee present at any annual meeting of the same.

Sec. 3. The officers of each Branch Society shall consist of a President, not less than ten Vice-Presidents, a Recording Secretary, a Corresponding Secretary, a Treasurer, an Auditor, and not less than ten Managers. These, with the exception of Auditor, shall constitute an Executive Committee for the administration of the affairs of the Branch, nine of whom shall be a quorum for the transaction of business. These officers shall be elected at the annual meeting of the Branch, and shall continue in office until others are chosen in their stead.

Sec. 4. The President, or one of the Vice-Presidents, shall preside at all meetings of the Branch and of its Executive Committee. The Recording Secretary shall notify all meetings of the Branch and of the Executive Committee, and shall keep a full record of the proceedings.

The Corresponding Secretary shall, under the direction of the Executive Committee, conduct the correspondence of the Society with foreign missionaries, with the other Branches, and with its auxiliary Societies hereinafter mentioned), and shall endeavor, by all practicable means, to form auxiliary Societies within the prescribed territory of the Branch. It shall also be her duty to present to the annual meeting of the General Executive Committee a report of the work of the Branch during the year, for publication in their Annual Report.

The Treasurer shall receive all contributions to the Branch, keeping proper books of account, and shall make such disposition of the funds as the Executive Committee may direct, each order of the Committee being duly signed by the Corresponding Secretary.

Sec. 5. The Executive Committee shall have full supervision of all the work assigned to the Branch by the General Executive Committee, and may order the disbursement of those funds required for that work, provide for all the wants and receive all the reports of the missionaries, Bible-women and teachers, who, by the plan of the General Executive Committee, are to be supported by their Branch.

Sec. 6. No Branch shall project new work or undertake the support of new missionaries, except by the direction or with the approval of the General Executive Committee.

Sec. 7. Each Branch may make its own by-laws regulating its meetings and those of its Executive Committee, also any others which may be deemed necessary to its efficiency not inconsistent with this Constitution.

Article VII.—Auxiliary Societies.

Any number of women who shall contribute not less than ten dollars annually may form a society auxiliary to that Branch of the Woman's Foreign Missionary Society of the Methodist Episcopal Church, within whose prescribed territorial limits they may reside, by appointing a President, three or more Vice-Presidents or Managers, a Recording Secretary, Corresponding Secretary, and Treasurer, who together shall constitute a local Executive Committee.

Article VIII.—Relation to the Missionary Authorities of the Church.

Section 1. This Society will work in harmony with and under the supervision of the authorities of the Missionary Society of the Methodist Episcopal Church, and be subject to their approval in the employment and remuneration of missionaries, the designation of their fields of labor, and in the general plans and designs of its work.

Sec. 2. All missionaries supported by the Society shall be approved by the constituted missionary authorities of the Methodist Episcopal Church, and shall labor under the direction of the authorities of the Missionary Society of the Methodist Episcopal Church and of the particular missions of the Society in which they may be severally employed; and they shall be subject to the same rules and regulations that govern the other missionaries in those particular missions.

Sec. 3. The funds of the Society shall not be raised by collections or subscriptions taken during any church services or in any promiscuous public meetings, but shall be raised by securing members, life-members, honorary managers and patrons, and by such other methods as will not interfere with the ordinary collections or contributions for the treasury of the Missionary Society of the Methodist Episcopal Church.

Article IX.—Change of Constitution.

This Constitution may be changed at any annual meeting of the General Executive Committee, by a two-thirds vote of each Branch delegation, notice of the proposed change having been given at the previous annual meeting; but Article VIII. shall not be changed except with the concurrence of the Board of Managers of the Missionary Society of the Methodist Episcopal Church.

BY-LAWS

OF THE GENERAL EXECUTIVE COMMITTEE.

1. The President and Corresponding Secretary of the Branch within whose precincts the meeting of the General Executive Committee is to be held, shall fix the exact date of the meeting of said Committee, and arrange for the anniversary exercises.

2. The Branch Corresponding Secretaries shall meet the day before the time of the meeting of the General Executive Committee, for the purpose of nominating the members of the Standing Committees, and planning work for its sessions, and report the same at the opening of said Committee.

3. The Corresponding Secretary of the Branch within whose bounds the Committee convenes shall preside over its meetings until a permanent organization is effected.

4. The Order of Business shall be as follows:

    1. Calling of the roll.

    2. Election of President and Secretary.

    3. Appointment of Standing Committees, i. e. Committee on Publication, Committee on Finance, Committee on Extension of Work, Committee on Application of Missionary Candidates.

    4. Reception of Reports from Corresponding Secretaries.

    5. Reception of Treasurers' Reports.

    6. Report of Committee of Reference.

    7. Report of Agent of HEATHEN WOMAN'S FRIEND.

    8. Presentation of information from foreign work.

    9. Reception of memorials, petitions and estimates.

    10. Fixing place of next meeting.

    11. Notices of constitutional amendments.

    12. Miscellaneous business.

13. Reports of Standing Committees, daily, immediately after "Reading of minutes."

5. The Rules of Order shall be as follows :

1. Each session shall open and close with devotional exercises.
2. All resolutions to be discussed shall be presented in writing.
3. All ladies speaking shall rise when they address the Chair.
4. No lady shall leave the room without permission from the Chair.

6. The Committee of Reference shall be composed of the Corresponding Secretaries of the various Branches, whose duties shall be as follows :

It shall hold correspondence with the missionaries in the different localities of our mission-field, in order that thorough information may be obtained with regard to all parts of our work—such information to be presented on requisition of the General Executive Committee; the fields of correspondence for the respective secretaries to be arranged by themselves.

It shall have power to adjust any matters of difference which may arise between the Branches, and to fill any vacancy that may occur in the office of the agent or editor of the HEATHEN WOMAN'S FRIEND during the year.

If a Branch Board desire to send a lady to a foreign field, the work having been estimated for by the General Executive Committee, her testimonials shall be sent to this Committee, and, a majority of them concurring, she may receive her appointment.

If it is deemed necessary to recall a missionary during the year, it shall have power to order her return.

If the office of treasurer in a foreign mission field become vacant during the year, it shall have power to fill the office.

7. The Branch Corresponding Secretaries shall superintend all the interests of their respective Branches ; shall conduct the correspondence of the Society with foreign missionaries ; shall be present at all Branch quarterly meetings and present a quarterly report of the work of the Branch, and shall give to the public, or direct to be given, all communications and plans of the business of their respective Branches.

8. The Secretary of each meeting of the General Executive Committee shall keep a full record of all proceedings, which, when entered upon a suitable book of record, shall be deposited in the safe of the HEATHEN WOMAN'S FRIEND, and shall be transmitted to the next meeting of the General Executive Committee by the Corresponding Secretary of the New England Branch.

9. These By-Laws may be amended at any meeting of the General Executive Committee by a two-thirds vote of the members present.

HISTORICAL SKETCH

— OF THE —

WOMAN'S FOREIGN MISSIONARY SOCIETY.

——o——

In the year 1860, in the city of New York, Mrs. T. C. Doremus, "mother of us all," founded the "Woman's Union Missionary Society for Heathen Lands." In 1868 "The Woman's Board of Missions, Auxiliary to the American Board," Congregational, was organized; in 1869 "The Woman's Foreign Missionary Society of the Methodist Episcopal Church"; in 1870 "The Woman's Missionary Society of the Presbyterian Church," and in 1871 "The Woman's Missionary Society of the Baptist Church" were severally organized and put into active operation. Since 1871 these five Societies have contributed to the cause of foreign missions an aggregate sum of $1,600,000.

As is so often the case in the beginning of great movements and inventions, this important enterprise had its origin in what was in itself a mere trifle. The wife of a missionary in India made a pair of slippers for her husband. A native gentleman saw and admired them, and desired the Christian woman to visit his home and teach his wife to make a pair for himself. At once the thought of what might be done for Christ by getting access to the homes of the better class of natives took possession of this devoted missionary; and as the two sewed the bright silks into the velvet, she prayerfully dropped into the heart of her pagan sister the seeds which developed into a Christian faith and life.

Our own Society was organized by Mrs. Rev. E. W. Parker, assisted by Mrs. Dr. William Butler, in Tremont Street Methodist Episcopal Church, Boston, March 22, 1869. The day was very stormy, and but nine ladies were present. In a letter bearing date March 20, Rev. Dr. Durbin, the Secretary of the Church Missionary Society, had advised the ladies, that in their contemplated organization they, first, raise funds for a particular portion of our mission work in India, possibly also in China; and, second, that they leave the administration of the work to the Board at home and the mission authorities abroad.

At a meeting of ladies, held March 30, a constitution embodying these recommendations was adopted, and the following elected the first official Board: Mrs. Bishop O. C. Baker, President; Mrs. William B. J. Pope, Recording Secretary. Mrs. William F. Warren, Mrs. E. W. Parker, and Mrs. J. F. Willing, Corresponding Secretaries; Mrs. Thomas A. Rich, Treasurer. Forty-four Vice-Presidents, representing the various States, and twelve Managers were also elected.

On May 7, in Boston, Drs. Durbin and Harris, Secretaries of the Missionary Society, met the representatives of the new organization, and after a full and free consultation officially approved the organization, and assumed the responsibility of communicating to the Church a statement of its plans and purposes; they also sanctioned the publication of a paper devoted to the cause of heathen women; and Dr. Harris received from the Treasurer the *first remittance* which was appropriated for the support of a native Bible-woman in India.

May 26, a meeting was held in Bromfield Street Methodist Episcopal Church, Boston, at which Gov. Claflin presided. The attendance was large; addresses were made by Dr. William F. Warren, of the Theological Seminary, Dr. Butler, and Rev. E. W. Parker, returned missionaries. Great enthusiasm was developed, and the ladies voted to send to India, as their first missionary, Miss Isabella Thoburn, of St. Clairsville, Ohio. In June of the same year appeared the first number of the paper, "THE HEATHEN WOMAN'S FRIEND." In July, through its columns came a call for a medical missionary to India; to which Miss Clara A. Swain, of Castile, N. Y., promptly responded; and Nov. 3, Misses Thoburn and Swain together sailed from New York for India.

Auxiliaries were rapidly formed, both in the east and west, and hundreds of ladies pledged themselves to the payment of two cents per week for the support of these missionaries. A plan was also adopted for dividing the territory to be worked into districts, similar to the mission districts of the Parent Society, and for organizing a Branch Society in each district. A General Executive Committee was also appointed, its duties in general terms defined, and its first meeting appointed for April 20, 1870.

The work of Branch organization went rapidly forward in the following order: Philadelphia Branch organized at the Book Rooms, Arch Street, March 3, 1870, Mrs. J. T. Gracey defining the objects and plans.

The New England Branch organized in Tremont Street Church, Boston,
... ... the New York Branch organized at the

the ladies of the Methodist Episcopal churches of that city organized "The
Ladies' China Missionary Society"; and for nearly a quarter of a century
they nobly sustained missionary work among the women of China. At
their Anniversary, March 6, 1871, they passed a resolution of co-operation
with the Woman's Foreign Missionary Society of the M. E. Church, and
on the 10th of the same month the Baltimore Branch was formally organized.

In the arrangement of districts, provision was made for the organization of Branches in the Southern and Pacific States; and at the meeting of
the General Executive Committee, held in Minneapolis, May, 1877, initial
steps were taken in this direction by the appointment of Mrs. C. B. Savage
and Mrs. J. P. Newman to the work of organization of Auxiliaries in our
churches in the Southern States.

The first General Executive Committee meeting was held as appointed,
April 20, 1870, and consisted of delegates from the six organized Branches,
save Cincinnati Branch, which was represented by Mrs. E. W. Parker.
At this meeting the Society adopted the regulations which, with slight
modification, control its present action.

The first Anniversary meeting occurred at 10 A. M., Thursday, April 21.
Mrs. Dr. Butler presiding. Reports were presented from each Corresponding Secretary present, a summary of which showed the work of the
first year to have been the endorsement of our Society by the Parent
Board and by the India Mission Conference, the successful opening of
Misses Thoburn and Swain's work at Lucknow and Bareilly, India; the
adoption of the Bareilly Orphanage; the opening of several Girls' and
Zenana Schools, and the employment of several Bible-women. Steps had
also been taken towards work in Foochow, Kiukiang and Peking, China.

But the most promising work of all reported for the year, was the up-
rising of the women all through the churches, filled with a new enthusiasm
for souls, and the spirit of consecration of both means and labor to their
salvation.

The following are the receipts of the Society for the successive years since its organization:

Total from organization, March 1, 1869, to Feb. 10, 1877. $379,798 98

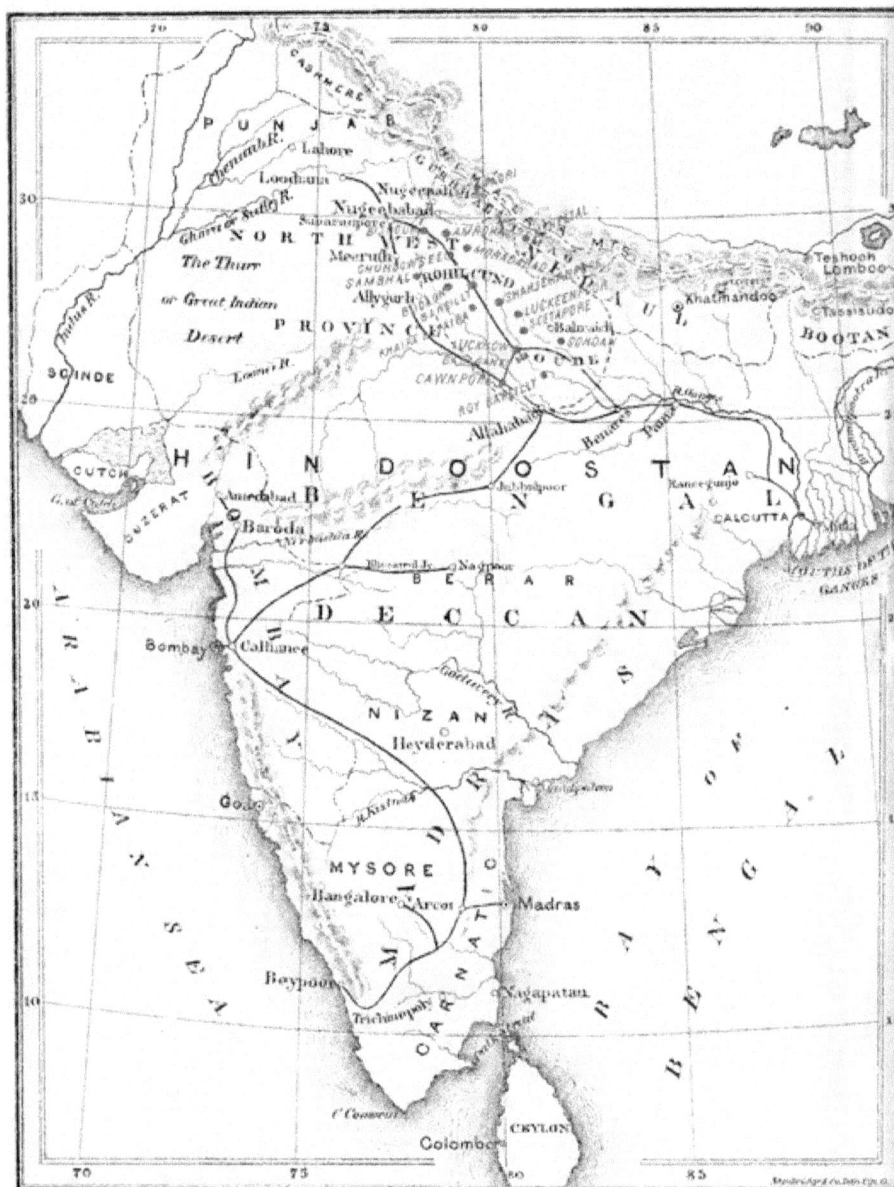

CASHMERE

PUNJAB

Chenaub R.
Lahore
Loodiana
Ghara or Sutlej R.
Nugeenah
Nugeenabad
NORTH WEST
Saharanpore
Meerudh
CHUNDOWSEE
SAMBHAL
Allygurh
KHAIR
PROVINCE
SUCKROW
ROY BAREILLY
CAWNPORE

The Thurr
or Great Indian
Desert
Lower R.

Indus R.

SCINDE

30

25

SANKISSA
GOOM
NANPAUL
AVULNEE
MORADABAD
ROHILCUND
SHAJEHANPORE
BARELLY
LUCKNOW
SEETAPORE
Balrumpeh
SONDAN
HIMALAYA MTS
Khatmandoo
Teshooh
Lomboo
Classisudoor
BOOTAN

MOUTHS OF THE
GANGES

Allahabad
Benares
Jumna
R.Goomtee

HINDOOSTAN
BENGAL
Ahmedabad
Baroda
Nerbudda R.
Jubbulpoor
Ranee-gunje
CALCUTTA

CUTCH
Gulf of Cutch
GUZERAT

20

Pewund Jr.
Nagpoor
BERAR

DECCAN
Bombay
Callumee
Goolburga
NIZAM
Heyderabad

GHAUTS

Goa
R.Kistnah

15

MYSORE
Bangalore
Arcot
Madras

BAY

OF

BENGAL

Beypoor
CARNATIC
Nagapatam
Trichinopoly

10

C. Comorin
CEYLON
Colombo

ARABIAN SEA